MASTER THE™ DSST®

Math for Liberal Arts Exam

About Peterson's

Peterson's® has been your trusted educational publisher for more than 50 years. It's a milestone we're quite proud of, as we continue to offer the most accurate, dependable, high-quality educational content in the field, providing you with everything you need to succeed. No matter where you are on your academic or professional path, you can rely on Peterson's for our books, online information, expert test-prep tools, the most up-to-date education exploration data, and the highest quality career success resources—everything you need to achieve your education goals. For our complete line of products, visit **www.petersons.com.**

For more information, contact Peterson's, 4380 S. Syracuse Street, Suite 200, Denver, CO 80237; 800-338-3282 Ext. 54229; or find us online at **www.petersons.com**.

ISBN: 978-0-7689-4416-7

Printed in the United States of America

10 9 8 7 6 5 4 3 2 1   23 22 21

Contents

Before You Begin

HOW THIS BOOK IS ORGANIZED

Peterson's *Master the™ DSST® Math for Liberal Arts Exam* provides a diagnostic test, subject-matter review, and a post-test.

- **Diagnostic Test**—Twenty multiple-choice questions, followed by an answer key with detailed answer explanations
- **Assessment Grid**—A chart designed to help you identify areas that you need to focus on based on your test results
- **Subject-Matter Review**—General overview of the exam subject, followed by a review of the relevant topics and terminology covered on the exam
- **Post-test**—Sixty multiple-choice questions, followed by an answer key and detailed answer explanations

The purpose of the diagnostic test is to help you figure out what you know—or don't know. The twenty multiple-choice questions are similar to the ones found on the DSST exam, and they should provide you with a good idea of what to expect. Once you take the diagnostic test, check your answers to see how you did. Included with each correct answer is a brief explanation regarding why a specific answer is correct, and in many cases, why other options are incorrect. Use the assessment grid to identify the questions you miss so that you can spend more time reviewing that information later. As with any exam, knowing your weak spots greatly improves your chances of success.

Following the diagnostic test is a subject-matter review. The review summarizes the various topics covered on the DSST exam. Key terms are defined; important concepts are explained; and when appropriate, examples are provided. As you read the review, some of the information may seem familiar while other information may seem foreign. Again, take note of the unfamiliar because that will most likely cause you problems on the actual exam.

After studying the subject-matter review, you should be ready for the post-test. The post-test contains sixty multiple-choice items, and it will serve as a dry run for the real DSST exam. There are complete answer explanations at the end of the test.

OTHER DSST® PRODUCTS BY PETERSON'S

Books, flashcards, practice tests, and videos available online at
www.petersons.com/testprep/dsst

- A History of the Vietnam War
- Art of the Western World
- Astronomy
- Business Mathematics
- Business Ethics and Society
- Civil War and Reconstruction
- Computing and Information Technology
- Criminal Justice
- Environmental Science
- Ethics in America
- Ethics in Technology
- Foundations of Education
- Fundamentals of College Algebra
- Fundamentals of Counseling
- Fundamentals of Cybersecurity
- General Anthropology
- Health and Human Development
- History of the Soviet Union
- Human Resource Management

- Introduction to Business
- Introduction to Geography
- Introduction to Geology
- Introduction to Law Enforcement
- Introduction to World Religions
- Lifespan Developmental Psychology
- Math for Liberal Arts
- Management Information Systems
- Money and Banking
- Organizational Behavior
- Personal Finance
- Principles of Advanced English Composition
- Principles of Finance
- Principles of Public Speaking
- Principles of Statistics
- Principles of Supervision
- Substance Abuse
- Technical Writing

Like what you see? Get unlimited access to Peterson's full catalog of DSST practice tests, instructional videos, flashcards, and more for **75% off the first month!** Go to **www.petersons.com/testprep/dsst** and use coupon code **DSST2020** at checkout. Offer expires July 1, 2021.

Chapter 1

All About the DSST® Exam

WHAT IS DSST®?

Previously known as the DANTES Subject Standardized Tests, the DSST program provides the opportunity for individuals to earn college credit for what they have learned outside of the traditional classroom. Accepted or administered at more than 1,900 colleges and universities nationwide and approved by the American Council on Education (ACE), the DSST program enables individuals to use the knowledge they have acquired outside the classroom to accomplish their educational and professional goals.

WHY TAKE A DSST® EXAM?

DSST exams offer a way for you to save both time and money in your quest for a college education. Why enroll in a college course in a subject you already understand? For more than 30 years, the DSST program has offered the perfect solution for individuals who are knowledgeable in a specific subject and want to save both time and money. A passing score on a DSST exam provides physical evidence to universities of proficiency in a specific subject. More than 1,900 accredited and respected colleges and universities across the nation award undergraduate credit for passing scores on DSST exams. With the DSST program, individuals can shave months off the time it takes to earn a degree.

The DSST program offers numerous advantages for individuals in all stages of their educational development:

- Adult learners
- College students
- Military personnel

Adult learners desiring college degrees face unique circumstances—demanding work schedules, family responsibilities, and tight budgets. Yet adult learners also have years of valuable work experience that can frequently be applied toward a degree through the DSST program. For example, adult learners with on-the-job experience in business and management might be able to skip the Business 101 courses if they earn passing marks on DSST exams such as Introduction to Business and Principles of Supervision.

Adult learners can put their prior learning into action and move forward with more advanced course work. Adults who have never enrolled in a college course may feel a little uncertain about their abilities. If this describes your situation, then sign up for a DSST exam and see how you do. A passing score may be the boost you need to realize your dream of earning a degree. With family and work commitments, adult learners often feel they lack the time to attend college. The DSST program provides adult learners with the unique opportunity to work toward college degrees without the time constraints of semester-long course work. DSST exams take two hours or less to complete. In one weekend, you could earn credit for multiple college courses.

The DSST exams also benefit students who are already enrolled in a college or university. With college tuition costs on the rise, most students face financial challenges. The fee for each DSST exam starts at $100 (plus administration fees charged by some testing facilities)—significantly less than the $750 average cost of a 3-hour college class. Maximize tuition assistance by taking DSST exams for introductory or mandatory course work. Once you earn a passing score on a DSST exam, you are free to move on to higher-level course work in that subject matter, take desired electives, or focus on courses in a chosen major.

Not only do college students and adult learners profit from DSST exams, but military personnel reap the benefits as well. If you are a member of the armed services at home or abroad, you can initiate your post-military career by taking DSST exams in areas with which you have experience. Military personnel can gain credit anywhere in the world, thanks to the fact that almost all of the tests are available through the internet at designated testing locations. DSST testing facilities are located at more than 500 military installations, so service members on active duty can get a jump-start on a post-military career with the DSST program. As an additional incentive, DANTES (Defense Activity for Non-Traditional Education Support) provides funding for DSST test fees for eligible members of the military.

More than 30 subject-matter tests are available in the fields of Business, Humanities, Math, Physical Science, Social Sciences, and Technology.

Available DSST® Exams

Business	Social Sciences
Business Ethics and Society	A History of the Vietnam War
Business Mathematics	Art of the Western World
Computing and Information Technology	Criminal Justice
Human Resource Management	Foundations of Education
Introduction to Business	Fundamentals of Counseling
Management Information Systems	General Anthropology
Money and Banking	History of the Soviet Union
Organizational Behavior	Introduction to Geography
Personal Finance	Introduction to Law Enforcement
Principles of Finance	Lifespan Developmental Psychology
Principles of Supervision	Substance Abuse
	The Civil War and Reconstruction

Humanities	Physical Sciences
Ethics in America	Astronomy
Introduction to World Religions	Environmental Science
Principles of Advanced English Composition	Health and Human Development
Principles of Public Speaking	Introduction to Geology

Math	Technology
Fundamentals of College Algebra	Ethics in Technology
Math for Liberal Arts	Fundamentals of Cybersecurity
Principles of Statistics	Technical Writing

As you can see from the table, the DSST program covers a wide variety of subjects. However, it is important to ask two questions before registering for a DSST exam.

1. Which universities or colleges award credit for passing DSST exams?
2. Which DSST exams are the most relevant to my desired degree and my experience?

Knowing which universities offer DSST credit is important. In all likelihood, a college in your area awards credit for DSST exams, but find out before taking an exam by contacting the university directly. Then review the list of DSST exams to determine which ones are most relevant to the degree you are seeking and to your base of knowledge. Schedule an appointment with your college adviser to determine which exams best fit your degree program and which college courses the DSST exams can replace. Advisers should also be able to tell you the minimum score required on the DSST exam to receive university credit.

DSST® TEST CENTERS

You can find DSST testing locations in community colleges and universities across the country. Check the DSST website (**www.getcollegecredit. com**) for a location near you or contact your local college or university to find out if the school administers DSST exams. Keep in mind that some universities and colleges administer DSST exams only to enrolled students. DSST testing is available to men and women in the armed services at more than 500 military installations around the world.

HOW TO REGISTER FOR A DSST® EXAM

Once you have located a nearby DSST testing facility, you need to contact the testing center to find out the exam administration schedule. Many centers are set up to administer tests via the internet, while others use printed materials. Almost all DSST exams are available as online tests, but the method used depends on the testing center. The cost for each DSST exam starts at $100, and many testing locations charge a fee to cover their costs for administering the tests. Credit cards are the only accepted payment method for taking online DSST exams. Credit card, certified check, and money order are acceptable payment methods for paper-and-pencil tests.

Test takers are allotted two score reports—one mailed to them and another mailed to a designated college or university, if requested. Online tests generate unofficial scores at the end of the test session, while individuals taking paper tests must wait four to six weeks for score reports.

PREPARING FOR A DSST® EXAM

Even though you are knowledgeable in a certain subject matter, you should still prepare for the test to ensure you achieve the highest score possible. The first step in studying for a DSST exam is to find out what will be on the specific test you have chosen. Information regarding test content is located on the DSST fact sheets, which can be downloaded at no cost from **www.getcollegecredit.com**. Each fact sheet outlines the topics covered on a subject-matter test, as well as the approximate percentage assigned to each topic. For example, questions on the Math for Liberal Arts exam are distributed in the following way: real number systems–11%, sets and logic–16%, metric system, conversions, and geometry–12%, algebra, graphs, and functions (as applied to real life applications)–11%, linear systems and inequalities–8%, exponents and logarithms, including financial literacy–22%, counting, probability theory, and statistics–20%.

In addition to the breakdown of topics on a DSST exam, the fact sheet also lists recommended reference materials. If you do not own the recommended books, then check college bookstores. Avoid paying high prices for new textbooks by looking online for used textbooks. Don't panic if you are unable to locate a specific textbook listed on the fact sheet; the textbooks are merely recommendations. Instead, search for comparable books used in university courses on the specific subject. Current editions are ideal, and it is a good idea to use at least two references when studying for a DSST exam. Of course, the subject matter provided in this book will be a sufficient review for most test takers. However, if you need additional information, then it is a good idea to have some of the reference materials at your disposal when preparing for a DSST exam.

Fact sheets include other useful information in addition to a list of reference materials and topics. Each fact sheet includes subject-specific sample questions like those you will encounter on the DSST exam. The sample questions provide an idea of the types of questions you can expect on the exam. Test questions are multiple-choice with one correct answer and three incorrect choices.

The fact sheet also includes information about the number of credit hours ACE has recommended be awarded by colleges for a passing DSST exam score. However, you should keep in mind that not all universities and colleges adhere to the ACE recommendation for DSST credit hours. Some institutions require DSST exam scores higher than the minimum score recommended by ACE. Once you have acquired appropriate reference materials and you have the outline provided on the fact sheet, you are ready to start studying, which is where this book can help.

TEST DAY

After reviewing the material and taking practice tests, you are finally ready to take your DSST exam. Follow these tips for a successful test day experience.

1. **Arrive on time.** Not only is it courteous to arrive on time to the DSST testing facility, but it also allows plenty of time for you to take care of check-in procedures and settle into your surroundings.

2. **Bring identification.** DSST test facilities require that candidates bring a valid government-issued identification card with a current photo and signature. Acceptable forms of identification include a current driver's license, passport, military identification card, or state-issued identification card. Individuals who fail to bring proper identification to the DSST testing facility will not be allowed to take an exam.

3. **Bring the right supplies.** If your exam requires the use of a calculator, you may bring a calculator that meets the specifications. For paper-based exams, you may also bring No. 2 pencils with an eraser and black ballpoint pens. Regardless of the exam methodology, you are NOT allowed to bring reference or study materials, scratch paper, or electronics such as cell phones, personal handheld devices, cameras, alarm wrist watches, or tape recorders to the testing center.

4. **Take the test.** During the exam, take the time to read each question and answer option carefully. Eliminate the choices you know are incorrect to narrow the number of potential answers. If a question completely stumps you, take an educated guess and move on—remember that DSSTs are timed; you will have 2 hours to take the exam.

With the proper preparation, DSST exams will save you both time and money. So join the thousands of people who have already reaped the benefits of DSST exams and move closer than ever to your college degree.

MATH FOR LIBERAL ARTS EXAM FACTS

The Math for Liberal Arts exam was developed to enable schools to award credit to students for knowledge equivalent to that learned by students taking the course. This exam covers topics such as real number systems; sets and logic; metric system, conversions and geometry; algebra, graphs and functions (as applied to real life applications); linear systems and inequalities; exponents and logarithms including financial literacy and counting, probability theory and statistics.

The DSST® Math for Liberal Arts exam consists of 80 multiple-choice questions to be answered in 2 hours. The use of a nonprogrammable calculator is permitted in this exam.

Area or Course Equivalent: Math for Liberal Arts
Level: Lower-level baccalaureate
Amount of Credit: 3 Semester Hours
Minimum Score: 400
Source: https://www.getcollegecredit.com/wp-content/assets/factsheets/MathForLiberalArts.pdf

I. Real Number Systems – 11%

   a. Real numbers: natural numbers; integers; rational and irrational numbers; the real number line. (percentages; fractions and reducing fractions; conversion between decimal numbers and fractions; operations with fractions, including distributive property)

   b. Operations with real numbers and their properties (including the distributive properties)

   c. Prime and composite numbers; divisibility rules; prime factors of composite numbers

   d. Systems of numeration: place value or positional value numeration; base 10 expanded forms; base 2 numbers; conversion between base 10 and base 2, including Roman numerals)

   e. Rules of exponents including rational exponents

   f. Scientific notation

II. Sets and Logic – 16%

a. The nature of sets

b. Subsets and set operations (set-builder notation; roster form, using sets to solve problems)

c. Using Venn diagrams to study set operations

d. Infinite sets

e. Simple and compound statements; qualifiers *and* and *or* and their symbols; conjunction and disjunction; conditional and biconditional statements including qualifiers

f. Truth value of a compound statement, including truth tables

g. Types of statements (negations of conditional statements and De Morgan's laws)

h. Logical arguments, including Euler circles

III. Metric System, Conversions, and Geometry – 12%

a. Introduction to metrics and US customary unit systems

b. Conversions between metric and US customary unit systems, including dimensional analysis

c. Properties of lines and angles

d. Perimeter and area of 2D geometric objects

e. Area, surface area, and volume of 3D solid objects

IV. Algebra, Graphs, and Functions (as applied to real life applications) – 11%

a. Order of operations

b. Simplifying expressions; equations with one variable; proportion problems

c. Evaluation of formulas

d. Graphs of linear equations in the rectangular coordinate system

e. Functions, including polynomials (not to include rational, exponential, and logarithmic functions)

V. Linear Systems and Inequalities – 8%

    a. Solving linear equations, including applications and systems

    b. The rectangular coordinate system and linear equations in two variables

    c. Graphing and solving linear inequalities

    d. Graphing and solving systems of inequalities

VI. Exponents and Logarithms, including Financial Literacy – 22%

    a. Properties of logarithms

    b. Logarithmic and exponential functions

    c. Simple interest

    d. Compound interest

    e. Installment buying

    f. Student loans and home buying

    g. Investing in stocks and bonds

VII. Counting, Probability Theory, and Statistics – 20%

    a. Fundamentals of probability, including the counting principle

    b. Permutations and combinations

    c. Events involving *not* and *or*

    d. Odds and conditional probability

    e. Mean, median, and mode

    f. Range, variance, and standard deviation

    g. Graphical representation (including bar graph, pie chart, histogram, line graph, scatterplots, etc.)

Chapter 2

Math for Liberal Arts Diagnostic Test

DIAGNOSTIC TEST ANSWER SHEET

1. Ⓐ Ⓑ Ⓒ Ⓓ

2. Ⓐ Ⓑ Ⓒ Ⓓ

3. Ⓐ Ⓑ Ⓒ Ⓓ

4. Ⓐ Ⓑ Ⓒ Ⓓ

5. Ⓐ Ⓑ Ⓒ Ⓓ

6. Ⓐ Ⓑ Ⓒ Ⓓ

7. Ⓐ Ⓑ Ⓒ Ⓓ

8. Ⓐ Ⓑ Ⓒ Ⓓ

9. Ⓐ Ⓑ Ⓒ Ⓓ

10. Ⓐ Ⓑ Ⓒ Ⓓ

11. Ⓐ Ⓑ Ⓒ Ⓓ

12. Ⓐ Ⓑ Ⓒ Ⓓ

13. Ⓐ Ⓑ Ⓒ Ⓓ

14. Ⓐ Ⓑ Ⓒ Ⓓ

15. Ⓐ Ⓑ Ⓒ Ⓓ

16. Ⓐ Ⓑ Ⓒ Ⓓ

17. Ⓐ Ⓑ Ⓒ Ⓓ

18. Ⓐ Ⓑ Ⓒ Ⓓ

19. Ⓐ Ⓑ Ⓒ Ⓓ

20. Ⓐ Ⓑ Ⓒ Ⓓ

MATH FOR LIBERAL ARTS DIAGNOSTIC TEST
24 minutes—20 questions

Directions: Carefully read each of the following 20 questions. Choose the best answer to each question and fill in the corresponding circle on the answer sheet. The Answer Key and Explanations can be found following this Diagnostic Test.

---

1. Write the following compound statement symbolically:
   "If I go to my personal trainer, then I will not overeat."

   > Let p represent "The food is delicious."
   > Let q represent "I will overeat."
   > Let s represent "I will go to my personal trainer."

   A. $q \Rightarrow s$
   B. $s \Rightarrow \sim q$
   C. $\sim (q \Rightarrow s)$
   D. $p \wedge q$

2. $\log\left(\dfrac{z}{1,000}\right) =$

   A. $3\log z$
   B. $\log(z - 1,000)$
   C. $3 + \log z$
   D. $-3 + \log z$

3. $8.48 \text{ m} = \underline{\hspace{2cm}} \text{ cm}$

   A. 0.0848
   B. 0.848
   C. 84.8
   D. 848

4. High school students who complete advanced course work in American History are invited to take an exam that will earn them college credit. The exam is scored on a scale of 1 to 5. The following represents the score distribution for a certain state.

Score	Percentage of Students Earning This Score
5	0.40
4	0.20
3	0.08
2	0.20
1	0.12

What is the mean exam score for this state?

A. 4.00

B. 3.56

C. 3.20

D. 3.00

5. What is the quotient of 6.9×10^7 and 2.3×10^3 expressed using scientific notation?

A. 3×10^3

B. 3×10^4

C. 3,000

D. 30,000

6. What is the value of the expression $4y - 3y^2x$ when $x = 2$ and $y = -4$?

A. 272

B. 80

C. −80

D. −112

7. The Junior Tennis League hosts an annual tournament in early summer. Eighty individuals are invited to participate in the tournament based on their rankings that year. After each round of matches, half of the individuals are eliminated. Which equation represents the number of individuals, I, that remain after m matches?

A. $I = 80(1.5)^m$
B. $I = 80(0.5)^m$
C. $I = 80(m)^{0.5}$
D. $I = 80(-0.5)^m$

8. If the probability of being selected for a paid internship is $\frac{1}{5}$, what are the odds of not being selected for the internship?

A. 4:5
B. 4:1
C. 1:4
D. 5:4

9. A survey conducted at a local gym shows that 70% of its patrons do aerobic exercise daily, 20% do strength-training exercises daily, and 10% do both daily. If a patron is selected at random, what is the probability that he or she does aerobic exercise or strength-training exercises daily?

A. 0.08
B. 0.10
C. 0.80
D. 0.90

10. The computing center at a university has purchased a new high-level server for $25,000. The value of the server, y, x years after its purchase is modeled by the linear function graphed below:

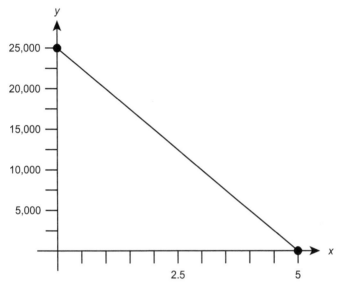

Determine the equation of this line and use it to predict the value of the server 2 years after purchase.

A. $y = -25,000x + 25,000$; value 2 years after purchase is $-\$25,000$
B. $y = -5,000x + 25,000$; value 2 years after purchase is $\$15,000$
C. $y = 5,000x - 25,000$; value 2 years after purchase is $\$15,000$
D. $y = 25,000x + 5$; value 2 years after purchase is $\$15,000$

11. Let p be the statement "The street is slippery" and q be the statement "The trees are losing their leaves." Which of the following is the truth table for the compound statement "The street is slippery or the trees are losing their leaves"?

A.

p	q	$p \vee q$
T	T	F
T	F	T
F	T	T
F	F	F

B.

p	q	$p \wedge q$
T	T	T
T	F	F
F	T	F
F	F	F

C.

p	q	$p \vee q$
T	T	T
T	F	T
F	T	T
F	F	F

D.

p	q	$p \wedge q$
T	T	T
T	F	F
F	T	F
F	F	T

12. The volume of a cylindrical container is 32π cubic centimeters. If the height of the container is 2 centimeters, what is the diameter of its base?

A. 2 centimeters

B. 4 centimeters

C. 8 centimeters

D. 16 centimeters

13. If *X* and *Y* are sets, which of the following Venn diagram correctly illustrates the set $X \cup Y$?

A.

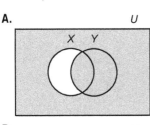

B.

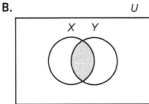

C.

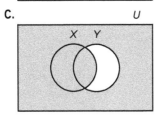

D.

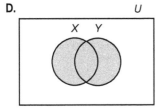

14. Erica invested $4,500 in a money market account that earns 3% interest compounded annually. She allowed the interest earned to be rolled into the account at the end of each year, but made no additional withdrawals from or deposits into this account. Which of these expressions can be used to determine the value of the account at the end of 4 years?

A. $4,500(1 + 0.03)^4$
B. $4,500(1 + 0.04)^3$
C. $4,500(1 + 0.3)^4$
D. $4,500(1 + 0.4)^3$

15. To which of the following systems of inequalities is this the solution set?

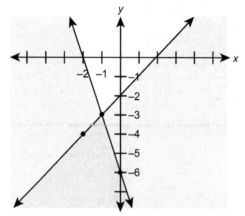

A. $\begin{cases} y \geq x + 3 \\ y \geq 2x - 6 \end{cases}$

B. $\begin{cases} y \leq x - 2 \\ y \leq -3x - 6 \end{cases}$

C. $\begin{cases} y \geq x - 2 \\ y \leq -3x - 6 \end{cases}$

D. $\begin{cases} y \leq x + 3 \\ y \leq 2x - 6 \end{cases}$

16. Three identical circular chips, one side of which is red and the other black, are tossed 80 times. The number of red sides is counted for each of these tosses, and the results of the experiment are recorded below. Based on this experiment, what is the probability that *at most* two red chips occur?

Number of Red Sides Occurring for a Toss	Frequency
0	10
1	8
2	12
3	50

A. $\dfrac{1}{8}$

B. $\dfrac{5}{8}$

C. $\dfrac{3}{8}$

D. $\dfrac{3}{20}$

17. What is the equivalent base 10 numeral for 10010000_2?

A. 20,020,000

B. 288

C. 144

D. 4

18. The set $A = \{x : x$ is a multiple of 3 that is larger than 5 and smaller than 20$\}$ has _____ elements.

A. 3

B. 5

C. 6,280

D. infinitely many

19. Jeffrey takes out a small student loan of $1,000 for 18 months at 11.5% APR to pay for books for a year. What is the finance charge?

   A. $60.75
   B. $93.50
   C. $1,060.75
   D. $1,093.50

20. Which of the following expressions is used to convert 90 kilometers per hour to meters per minute?

   A. $\dfrac{90 \text{ km}}{1 \text{ hr}} \times \dfrac{1,000 \text{ m}}{1 \text{ km}} \times \dfrac{1 \text{ hr}}{60 \text{ min}}$

   B. $\dfrac{90 \text{ km}}{1 \text{ hr}} \times \dfrac{1,000 \text{ m}}{1 \text{ km}} \times \dfrac{60 \text{ min}}{1 \text{ hr}}$

   C. $\dfrac{90 \text{ km}}{1 \text{ hr}} \times \dfrac{1 \text{ km}}{1,000 \text{ m}} \times \dfrac{60 \text{ min}}{1 \text{ hr}}$

   D. $\dfrac{90 \text{ km}}{1 \text{ hr}} \times \dfrac{1 \text{ km}}{1,000 \text{ m}} \times \dfrac{1 \text{ hr}}{60 \text{ min}}$

ANSWER KEY AND EXPLANATIONS

1. B	5. B	9. C	13. D	17. C
2. D	6. D	10. B	14. A	18. B
3. D	7. B	11. C	15. B	19. B
4. B	8. B	12. C	16. C	20. A

1. **The correct answer is B.** The given statement is a conditional (if-then) statement. The hypothesis is s and the conclusion is the negation of q, or $\sim q$. So, symbolically, this statement can be written as $s \Rightarrow \sim q$. Choice A is equivalent to "If I will overeat, then I will go to my personal trainer." In choice C, $\sim (q \Rightarrow s) \equiv \sim (\sim q \vee s) \equiv q \wedge \sim s$, which is the statement "I will overeat and I will not go to my personal trainer." Choice D is equivalent to "The food is delicious and I will overeat."

2. **The correct answer is D.** Use the logarithm property governing quotients and simplify to get $\log\left(\dfrac{z}{1000}\right) = \log z - \log 1{,}000 = \log z - 3 = -3 + \log z$. Choice A is incorrect because the logarithm of a quotient is the difference of the logarithms of the inputs, not their product. Choice B is incorrect because the logarithm of a quotient is the difference of the logarithms of the input, not the logarithm of the difference of the inputs. Choice C is incorrect because the logarithm of a quotient is not the sum of the logarithms of the inputs.

3. **The correct answer is D.** Since 1 m = 100 cm, it follows that 8.48 m = 8.48(100) cm = 848 cm. Choices A and B moved the decimal point in the wrong direction, while choice C did not move the decimal point enough places to the right.

4. **The correct answer is B.** To compute the mean, multiply each score by the percentage of students receiving that score, and then sum the products: $5(0.40) + 4(0.20) + 3(0.08) + 2(0.20) + 1(0.12) = 3.56$. Choice A is the median score. Choice C is the result of an arithmetic error. Choice D is the middle score that students can earn, but based on the percentages provided, it is not the mean (arithmetic) score.

5. **The correct answer is B.** Divide the decimal parts and the powers of ten separately:

$$\frac{6.9 \times 10^7}{2.3 \times 10^3} = \frac{6.9 \times 10^7}{2.3 \times 10^3}$$
$$= 3 \times 10^{7-3}$$
$$= 3 \times 10^4$$

Choice A is one power of 10 off from the correct quotient. Choices C and D are not expressed using scientific notation.

6. **The correct answer is D.** Substitute $x = 2$ and $y = -4$ into the expression and simplify using the order of operations:

$$4(-4) - 3(-4)^2(2) = -16 - 3(16)(2) = -16 - 96 = -112$$

Choice A is the result of an arithmetic error. Choices B and C are the results of sign errors arising when computing products of integers with different signs.

7. **The correct answer is B.** Before the first match, there are 80 individuals. Following the first match, there are half as many individuals in the match, namely $80(0.5)$.

After the second match, there are half of this number, namely $80(0.5)(0.5) = 80(0.5)^2$. So, after m matches, the number of individuals who remain in the tournament is $80(0.5)^m$. Choice A has the number of individuals who remain in the tournament *increasing* the more matches that are played. Choice C has m and 0.5 interchanged. Choice D yields a negative number of individuals for any odd number of matches played.

8. **The correct answer is B.** Let A be the event "being selected for the internship." We are given that $P(A) = \frac{1}{5}$. So, the probability of *not* being selected for the internship is $P(\text{not } A) = \frac{4}{5}$.

The odds of *not* being selected for the internship are:

$$\frac{P(\text{not } A)}{1 - P(\text{not } A)} = \frac{\frac{4}{5}}{1 - \frac{4}{5}} = \frac{\frac{4}{5}}{\frac{1}{5}} = \frac{4}{1}, \text{ which can be written as 4:1.}$$

Choice A is the probability of not getting the internship incorrectly written in the form of an odds ratio. Choice C is nearly correct, but written backwards. Choice D is the reciprocal of the probability of not getting the internship incorrectly written in the form of an odds ratio.

9. **The correct answer is C.** Let A be the event "patron does aerobic exercise daily" and B be the event "patron does strength-training exercises daily." Then, $A \cap B$ is the event "patron does both types of exercise daily" and $A \cup B$ is the event "patron does aerobic exercise *or* strength-training exercise daily." Using the addition formula yields

$$P(A \cup B) = P(A) + P(B) - P(A \cap B)$$
$$= 0.70 + 0.20 - 0.10$$
$$= 0.80$$

Choice A is incorrect because of an arithmetic error made when working with decimals. Choice B is the probability that the patron does *both* types of exercise daily, not *either type*. Choice D is the result of subtracting the probability that the patron does *both* types of exercise daily when applying the addition formula.

10. **The correct answer is B.** The y-intercept, apparent from the graph, is 25,000. The slope of the line is $\frac{25,000 - 0}{0 - 5} = -5,000$. The equation of the line is $y = -5,000x + 25,000$. Using this line with $x = 2$ yields the value after 2 years as \$15,000. Choice A is incorrect because the slope of the line is −5,000 not −25,000. Choices C and D cannot be correct because their slopes are positive, but the graph of the line is decreasing and so has a negative slope.

11. **The correct answer is C.** The given statement is a disjunction (or) statement. This immediately eliminates choices B and D. Of the remaining answer options, choice C is correct because only one statement needs to be true for the "or" statement to be true. The only way for the "or" statement to be false is for both statements to be false.

12. **The correct answer is C.** Let r be the radius, h the height, and V the volume of the cylinder. Substituting the given information into the volume formula $V = \pi r^2 h$ yields the equation $32\pi = \pi r^2(2)$. This is equivalent to $r^2 = 16$, so that $r = 4$. As such, the diameter is 8 centimeters. Choice A is the height, not the radius. Choice B is the radius. Choice D is twice the diameter.

13. **The correct answer is D.** The union of two sets X and Y is the set of elements that belong to either X or Y or to both. The portion shaded in the Venn diagram in choice D shows this set. Choice A is incorrect because it shows the union of Y and the complement of X. Choice B is incorrect because it shows the intersection of X and Y. Choice C is incorrect because it shows the union of X and the complement of Y.

14. **The correct answer is A.** The account starts at $4,500. After one year, 3% interest is earned, which results in the account being worth $4,500 + \$4,500(0.03) = \$4,500(1 + 0.03)$ at the end of one year. This amount is now invested in the account and earns 3% interest at the end of the second year. This results in the account being worth:

$$\$4,500(1 + 0.03) + [\$4,500(1 + 0.03)](0.03) =$$
$$\$4,500(1 + 0.03)\{1 + 0.03\} = \$4,500 \ (1 + 0.03)^2.$$

Continuing this process for the third and then fourth years yields the value of the account at the end of four years being $4,500(1 + 0.03)^4$.

Choice B is incorrect because the expression has the 3 and 4 reversed. Choice C incorrectly has the interest rate as 30%, not 3%. In choice D, not only are the 3 and 4 reversed, but there is an additional percentage error resulting in a 40% interest rate.

15. The correct answer is B. First, find the equations of both lines. The slope of the line that is rising from left to right is $m = \dfrac{-3 - (-4)}{-1 - (-2)} = 1$. Using the point-slope formula with the point $(-2, -4)$ yields the equation $y - (-4) = 1(x - (-2))$, which is equivalent to $y = x - 2$. Since the region *below* this line is shaded, one inequality of the system must be $y \leq x - 2$. The slope of the other line is $\dfrac{-3 - (-6)}{-1 - 0} = 3$. Since the y-intercept is -6, the equation of this line is $y = -3x - 6$. Since the region *below* this line is shaded, one inequality of the system must be $y \leq -3x - 6$. Thus, the system of inequalities for which the shaded region is the solution set is given by choice B. Choices A and D have incorrect equations. Choice C has the inequality sign reversed in the top equation.

16. The correct answer is C. The event "*at most* 2 red chips" is satisfied if there are 0 red chips, 1 red chip, or 2 red chips on a toss. Adding those entries and dividing by 80 total tosses yields $\dfrac{30}{80} = \dfrac{3}{8}$. Choice A is the probability of getting 0 red chips. Choice B is the probability of getting more than 2 red chips. Choice D is the probability of getting exactly 2 red chips.

17. The correct answer is C. Using the place-value chart for base 2 shows that

2^7	1
2^6	0
2^5	0
2^4	1
2^3	0
2^2	0
2^1	0
2^0	0

So, the base 10 equivalent of 10010000_2 is $2^7 + 2^4 = 144$. Choice A is equivalent to the product of 1001000 and 2; this is not how you convert a base 2 numeral to a base 10 numeral. Choice B is equivalent to 100100000_2 (one extra zero at the end of the numeral). Choice D is equivalent to 100_2.

18. **The correct answer is B.** The multiples of 3 that are larger than 5 but smaller than 20 are 6, 9, 12, 15, and 18. Therefore, there are 5 elements in the set. Choice A is incorrect since it just counts the 3, 5, and 20 as elements. Choice C is incorrect since it counts 3 along with the other elements (but 3 is not in the set since it is smaller than 5). Finally, choice D is incorrect since there is a finite set of numbers with these properties.

19. **The correct answer is B.** Using the formula $R = \dfrac{A \times i}{\left(1 - \dfrac{1}{(1+i)^n}\right)}$,

where A is the amount of the loan, R is the monthly payment, i is the monthly interest rate (= APR/12), and n is the total number of payments, with $A = \$1,000$, $i = \dfrac{0.115}{12}$, and $n = 18$ yields:

$$R = \frac{1,000 \times \dfrac{0.115}{12}}{\left(1 - \dfrac{1}{\left(1 + \dfrac{0.115}{12}\right)^{18}}\right)} = 60.75$$

The total amount Jeffrey pays is $\$60.75(18) = \$1,093.50$. The total finance charge is $\$1,093.50 - \$1,000 = \$93.50$. Choice A is the monthly payment. Choice C is the original loan amount plus a monthly payment. Choice D is the total amount paid.

20. **The correct answer is A.** Two units need to be converted: (1) kilometers to meters and (2) hours to minutes. The end result must have m in the numerator (with km canceling) and min in the denominator (with hours canceling). This is given by the following:

$$\frac{90 \text{ km}}{1 \text{ hr}} \times \frac{1,000 \text{ m}}{1 \text{ km}} \times \frac{1 \text{ hr}}{60 \text{ min}}$$

Choice B is incorrect because hours does not cancel. Choice C is incorrect because neither kilometers nor hours cancel. Choice D is incorrect because kilometers does not cancel.

DIAGNOSTIC TEST ASSESSMENT GRID

Now that you've completed the diagnostic test and read through the answer explanations, you can use your results to target your studying. Find the question numbers from the diagnostic test that you answered incorrectly and highlight or circle them below. Then focus extra attention on the sections dealing with those topics.

Math for Liberal Arts

Content Area	Topic	Question #
Real Number Systems	• Real numbers: natural numbers, integers, rational numbers, irrational numbers, the real number line • Operations with real numbers and their properties (including the distributive properties) • Prime and composite numbers, divisibility rules, prime factors of composite numbers • Systems of numeration: place value or positional value numeration, base 10 expanded forms, base 2 numbers, conversion between base 10 and base 2, (including roman numerals) • Rules of exponents, including rational exponents • Scientific notation	5, 17
Sets and Logic	• The nature of sets • Subsets and set operations • Using Venn diagrams • Infinite sets • Simple and compound statements • Truth value • Types of statements • Logical arguments	1, 11, 13, 18
Metric System, Conversions, and Geometry	• Introduction to metrics and US customary unit systems • Conversions between metric and US customary unit systems, including dimensional analysis • Properties of lines and angles • Perimeter and area of 2D geometric objects • Area, surface area, and volume of 3D solid objects	3, 12, 20

Algebra, Graphs, and Functions	• Order of operations • Simplifying expressions; equations with one variable; proportion problems • Evaluation of formulas • Graphs of linear equations in the rectangular coordinate system • Functions including polynomials (not to include rational, exponential, and logarithmic functions)	6, 10
Linear Systems and Inequalities	• Solving linear equations including applications and systems • The rectangular coordinate system and linear equations in two variables • Graphing and solving linear inequalities • Graphing and solving systems of inequalities	15
Exponents, Logarithms, and Financial Literacy	• Properties of logarithms • Logarithmic and exponential Functions • Simple interest • Compound interest • Installment buying • Student loans and home buying • Investing in stocks and bonds	2, 7, 14, 19
Counting, Probability Theory, and Statistics	• Fundamentals of probability, including the counting principle • Permutations and combinations • Events involving not and or • Odds and conditional probability • Mean, median, and mode • Range, variance, and standard deviation • Graphical representation (including bar graph, pie chart, histogram, line graph, scatterplots, etc.)	4, 8, 9, 16

Chapter 3

Math for Liberal Arts Subject Review

OVERVIEW

- Real Number Systems
- Sets and Logic
- Metric System, Conversions, and Geometry
- Algebra, Graphs, and Functions
- Linear Systems and Inequalities
- Exponents, Logarithms, and Financial Literacy
- Counting, Probability Theory, and Statistics
- Summing It Up

REAL NUMBER SYSTEMS

In this section, we'll review the basic arithmetic and properties of real numbers, along with two other commonly used numeration systems. The information covered by real number systems will serve you well when approaching every math problem on your exam—it is the foundation of even the most complex problems.

> **NOTE:** Around 11 percent of the questions on the DSST Math for Liberal Arts exam are devoted to real number systems.

Real Numbers

Natural Numbers

The set of **natural numbers** consists of the numbers 1, 2, 3, 4... The result when at least two natural numbers are multiplied is called a **product** and each number in the list being multiplied is a **factor** or **divisor**. A natural number is a **multiple** of each of its factors.

- For instance, in the expression $2 \times 5 \times 7 = 70$, 70 is the product; 2, 5, and 7 are factors of 70; and 70 is a multiple of 2, 5, and 7.

A natural number other than 1 is **prime** if it can only be written as a product of itself and 1; otherwise, it is **composite**.

Every composite number can be written as a product of prime numbers; the product is the **prime factorization** of the number.

- For instance, $56 = 2 \times 2 \times 2 \times 7$, or more succinctly, $56 = 2^3 \times 7$.

The following divisibility rules are useful when determining factors of a natural number.

Natural Number	A natural number n is divisible by the number in the left column if...
2	The number n ends in 0, 2, 4, 6, or 8.
3	The digit sum of n (i.e., the sum of all digits in the numeral n) is divisible by 3.
4	The last two numbers of n, taken as a number in and of itself, is divisible by 4.
5	The number n ends in 0 or 5.
6	The number n is divisible by both 2 and 3.
9	The digit sum of n is divisible by 9.
10	The number n ends in 0.

For instance, 459 is divisible by 3 because the digit sum $(4 + 5 + 9 = 18)$ is divisible by 3. The **greatest common factor (GCF)** of two natural numbers x and y is the *largest* natural number that is a factor of both x and y, while the **least common multiple (LCM)** of x and y is the *smallest* natural number that is a multiple of both x and y.

- For instance, the GCF of 32 and 56 is 8 and the LCM is 224.

Integers

The set of integers is comprised of the natural numbers, their negatives, and 0: {..., −3, −2, −1, 0, 1, 2, 3...}.

The following rules and terminology are useful when working with integers:

- $-(-a) = a$, for any integer a.
- $a - (-b) = a + b$, for any integers a, b.
- A product of two negative integers is positive.
- A product of one positive and one negative integer is negative.
- An integer is *even* if it is a multiple of 2, while it is *odd* if it is not a multiple of 2. Any even number can be written as $2n$, where n is an integer, and an odd number can be written as $2n + 1$, where n is an integer.

Exponent Rules

If b and n are natural numbers, then $b^n = b \times ... \times b$ for n times.

Suppose that a, b, m, and n are all real numbers. The following properties hold:

Example 1: $b^m b^n = b^{m+n}$

Example 2: $\dfrac{b^m}{b^n} = b^{m-n}$

Example 3: $(ab)^m = a^m b^m$

Example 4: $\left(\dfrac{a}{b}\right)^m = \dfrac{a^m}{b^m}$

Example 5: $\left(b^m\right)^n = b^{m \cdot n}$

Example 6: $b^0 = 1$, provided b is not zero

Example 7: $b^{-n} = \dfrac{1}{b^n}$

Example 8: $\dfrac{1}{b^{-n}} = b^n$

Example 9: $b^{\frac{n}{m}} = \sqrt[m]{b^n}$

The following are some examples that demonstrate how these properties can be used to simplify various expressions involving exponents. They apply not only to arithmetic expressions, but also to algebraic expressions: the latter are discussed more thoroughly later in this chapter.

$$\frac{2}{5 \cdot 3^{-2}} \underset{(E8)}{=} \frac{2 \cdot 3^2}{5} = \frac{2 \cdot 9}{5} = \frac{18}{5}$$

$$\left(\frac{3}{2x^{-3}}\right)^2 \underset{(E8)}{=} \left(\frac{3x^3}{2}\right)^2 \underset{(E4)}{=} \frac{\left(3x^3\right)^2}{2^2} \underset{(E3)}{=} \frac{3^2\left(x^3\right)^2}{2^2} \underset{(E5)}{=} \frac{9x^6}{4}$$

$$\left(\frac{4x^{-3}y^{-1}z}{2x^{-1}yz^{-3}}\right)^{-2} \underset{(E7),(E8)}{=} \left(\frac{4xzz^3}{2x^3yy}\right)^{-2} \underset{(E1)}{=} \left(\frac{4z^4}{2x^2y^2}\right)^{-2} \underset{(E4),(E3)}{=} \frac{4^{-2}z^{-8}}{2^{-2}x^{-4}y^{-4}} \underset{(E7),(E8)}{=} \frac{2^2x^4y^4}{4^2z^8} = \frac{4x^4y^4}{16z^8} = \frac{x^4y^4}{4z^8}$$

TIP: Remember, you cannot divide by 0!

Rational Numbers and Irrational Numbers

A **rational number** is a quotient of two integers, denoted by $\frac{a}{b}$, where $b \neq$ 0. Such a fraction is **simplified** if a and b do not share common factors. If $a \neq 0$, the **reciprocal** of $\frac{a}{b}$ can be computed by flipping the fraction over to get $\frac{b}{a}$. To get the reciprocal of a mixed number, first convert it to an **improper fraction** (one with a numerator greater than its denominator) and flip *that* fraction over. The arithmetic rules for working with fractions are as follows:

TIP: The complex fraction $\dfrac{\frac{a}{b}}{\frac{c}{d}}$ means $\frac{a}{b} \div \frac{c}{d}$.

Arithmetic Operation	Rule (in symbols)	What To Do (in words)
Cancellation Property	$\dfrac{a \cdot b}{b \cdot c} = \dfrac{a}{c}$	Factors common to numerator and denominator can be canceled.
Sum/Difference (same denominator)	$\dfrac{a}{b} - \dfrac{c}{b} = \dfrac{a \pm c}{b}$	Just add or subtract the numerators.
Sum/Difference (different denominators)	$\dfrac{a}{b} - \dfrac{c}{d} = \dfrac{ad - cb}{bd}$	First get a common denominator. Apply it to the fractions and then add the numerators.

Multiply by −1	$-\dfrac{a}{b} = \dfrac{-a}{b} = \dfrac{a}{-b}$	You can multiply either the numerator or denominator by −1, but NOT both.
Product	$\dfrac{a}{b} \times \dfrac{c}{d} = \dfrac{ac}{bd}$	Multiply numerators and denominators, though it is better to simplify first.
Quotient	$\dfrac{a}{b} \div \dfrac{c}{d} = \dfrac{a}{b} \cdot \dfrac{d}{c} = \dfrac{ad}{bc}$	Convert to a multiplication problem, and then multiply as above.

When performing arithmetic operations involving fractions, simplifying all fractions *first* will lead to smaller numbers which makes working out your calculations easier.

Operations with Real Numbers and their Properties

As the name implies, an **irrational number** is a real number that is not rational. An irrational number is a real number that cannot be written as a simple fraction. Some common examples are square roots of prime numbers, π, and e. Irrational numbers can be formed by performing arithmetic combinations of pairs of rational and irrational numbers:

- The sum of two positive irrational numbers is a positive irrational number.
- The sum of two negative irrational numbers is a negative irrational number.
- The product of a nonzero rational number and an irrational number is an irrational number.
- The sum or difference of a rational number and an irrational number is an irrational number.

The sets of rational numbers and irrational numbers both possess the so-called **density property**. This means that between *any* two rational (or irrational) numbers, there is another rational number and an irrational number. In fact, there are *infinitely many*. This can be counterintuitive, especially when the two rational (or irrational) numbers are very close together. For instance, what is a rational number between $\dfrac{1}{10,000}$ and $\dfrac{1}{10,001}$?

Using the fact that sums and quotients of rational numbers are again rational, the arithmetic average of these two numbers is a rational number halfway between them: $\dfrac{\dfrac{1}{10,000} + \dfrac{1}{10,001}}{2} = \dfrac{\dfrac{20,001}{100,010,000}}{2} = \dfrac{20,001}{200,020,000}$.

The following properties apply *for all* real numbers a, b, and c:

Property Name	Rule (in symbols)	What To Do (in words)
Commutative	$a + b = b + a$ $a \times b = b \times a$	The order in which real numbers are added or multiplied does not affect the outcome.
Associative	$(a + b) + c = a + (b + c)$ $(a \cdot b) \cdot c = a \cdot (b \cdot c)$	The way terms of a sum or a product comprised of more than two terms are grouped does not affect the outcome.
Distributive	$a \cdot (b + c) = a \cdot b + a \cdot c$	To multiply a sum by a real number, multiply each term of the sum by the number and add the results.
Identity	$a + 0 = 0 + a = a$ $a \cdot 1 = 1 \cdot a = a$	If you add 0 to a real number or multiply the real number by 1, the result is the same real number.
Zero Factor Property	If $a \cdot b = 0$, then either $a = 0$ or $b = 0$, or both $= 0$.	If a product of real numbers is zero, then at least one of the factors must be zero.

TIP: Using the distributive property twice shows how to multiply two binomials: $(a + b)(c + d) = ac + ad + bc + bd$. The acronym FOIL (first, outer, inner, last) shows all combinations of terms to be multiplied.

Decimals

Decimals are comprised of numerals appearing before and after a decimal point, each which represents a multiple of a power of 10. A place-value chart is useful when interpreting a decimal.

For example, 3,320.4461 is interpreted as follows:

10^4	10^3	10^2	10^1	10^0	•	10^{-1}	10^{-2}	10^{-3}	10^{-4}	10^{-5}
	3	3	2	0	•	4	4	6	1	

$$3{,}320.4461 = (3 \times 10^3) + (3 \times 10^2) + (2 \times 10^1) + (0 \times 10^0) + (4 \times 10^{-1}) +$$
$$(4 \times 10^{-2}) + (6 \times 10^{-3}) + (1 \times 10^{-4})$$

To convert 3,320.4461 to a fraction, note the following:

$$(4 \times 10^{-1}) + (4 \times 10^{-2}) + (6 \times 10^{-3}) + (1 \times 10^{-4})$$
$$= \frac{4}{10} + \frac{4}{100} + \frac{6}{1{,}000} + \frac{1}{10{,}000} = \frac{4{,}461}{10{,}000}$$

As such, 3,320.4461 is equal to the mixed number $3{,}320 \, \frac{4.461}{10{,}000}$, which is

subsequently equal to the improper fraction $\frac{33{,}204{,}461}{10{,}000}$. As in this case,

representing a decimal as a fraction will not always be in its simplest form, but it is nonetheless the fraction equivalent to the decimal. Likewise, any rational number can be converted into a decimal by dividing its numerator by its denominator. Such decimals will either terminate or repeat. Irrational numbers, like π and e, have decimal representations that neither terminate nor repeat—meaning it is impossible to list all the digits of such a decimal.

The arithmetic of decimals is the same as for natural numbers, with the additional step of correctly positioning the decimal point. The following are some rules of thumb to apply when working with decimals:

- When *adding or subtracting* decimals, line up the decimal points and add or subtract as you would natural numbers, keeping the decimal point in the same position.
- When *multiplying* decimals, first multiply the numbers as you would natural numbers. To determine the position of the decimal point, count the number of digits present to the right of the decimal point in all numbers being multiplied and move that many steps to the left. Start at the end of the product and place the decimal point in the correct position.

Scientific Notation

Real numbers that cannot be conveniently written in decimal form are expressed using scientific notation: this is the form $m \times 10^n$, where m is a decimal with a single nonzero digit appearing before the decimal point and n is an integer. The following are some basic rules for working with scientific notation:

- To convert from scientific notation to decimal form, remove the "$\times 10^n$" portion by shifting the decimal point n places to the right (if $n > 0$) or n places to the left (if $n < 0$).
- To convert from decimal form to scientific notation, move the decimal point n places (to the left if there is more than a single digit before the decimal point, or to the right if there are no nonzero digits appearing before the decimal point). Then, append "$\times 10n$" to the right of the decimal. The exponent n will be negative if the decimal point was moved to the right n places, and will be positive if it was moved to the left n places.

Suppose $m_2 x = m_1 \times 10^{n_1}$ and $y = m_2 \times 10^{n_2}$. Then, using the laws of exponents and the commutative and associative properties of real numbers, we can multiply and divide real numbers expressed in scientific notation as follows:

$$x \cdot y = (m_1 \times 10^{n_1}) \cdot (m_2 \times 10^{n_2}) = (m_1 \cdot m_2) \times (10^{n_1} \times 10^{n_2}) = (m_1 \cdot m_2) \times 10^{n_1 + n_2}$$

$$\frac{x}{y} = \frac{m_1 \times 10^{n_1}}{m_2 \times 10^{n_2}} = \left(\frac{m_1}{m_2}\right) \times \left(\frac{10^{n_1}}{10^{n_2}}\right) = \left(\frac{m_1}{m_2}\right) \times 10^{n_1 - n_2}$$

These products and quotients may need to be further converted to scientific notation form if the portion before the decimal point corresponding to $m_1 \cdot m_2$ and $\dfrac{m_1}{m_2}$ consists of anything but one digit.

Working with Percentages

A **percent** is used to express the number of parts of a whole. For instance, 34 percent means "34 parts of 100," which can be expressed as the fraction $\dfrac{34}{100}$, as the decimal 0.34, or using the notation 34%.

All three representations are equivalent. To go from decimal form to percent form, you simply move the decimal point two units to the right and affix the % sign; to convert in the opposite manner, move the decimal point two units to the left, insert a decimal point and drop the % sign.

To find a percent, divide part by whole. Algebraically, this would be percent(decimal form) = part/whole. You can rearrange this equation to also find the part and whole. To find the part, use part = percent(decimal form) × whole. And the whole value is found with whole = part/percent (decimal form).

These basic scenarios are represented below with variables and their common phrasings.

Question: What percent of x is y?

Answer: Divide y by x.

Question: Compute x% of y.

Answer: Convert x% to a decimal and multiply by y.

Question: x is y% of what number z?

Answer: Convert y% to a decimal and divide x by y (decimal form), which can be set equal to z.

The Real Number Line and Ordering

The **real number line** is a convenient way of illustrating the relative position of real numbers with respect to 0. This leads to the notion of **ordering**. What does it mean for a real number p to be *less than* a real number q, written $p < q$? Pictorially, q would be further to the right along the real number line than p. We also say that q is *greater than* p.

For instance:

$$-2 < -\frac{3}{5}$$

$$3.234 \leq 3.235$$

$$\pi \geq 3.14$$

$$0 > -0.0002$$

The following are some important properties involving inequalities of real numbers:

Rule (in symbols)	What To Do (in words)
If $0 < a < 1$, then $a^2 < a$.	Squaring a real number between 0 and 1 results in a smaller real number.
If $0 < a < b$, then $-b < -a < 0$.	If a and b are both positive and a is less than b, then the reverse inequality is true of the negatives of a and b.
If $a < b$ and $c < d$, then $a + c < b + d$.	If you add the left sides and right sides of inequalities involving the same sign, then the sums satisfy the same inequality.

Other Numeration Systems

Different numeration systems have been designed for specific purposes, while others arose as different civilizations' means of communicating numeracy. The base 2 (binary) system and Roman numerals are two well-known examples.

The familiar base 10 system involves expressing real numbers using powers of 10, and allows for digits 0, 1, 2, 3, 4, 5, 6, 7, 8, and 9 to occupy any space in the place-value system. Similarly, base 2 involves expressing real numbers using powers of 2, and allows for digits 0 or 1 to occupy any space in its place-value system.

Focusing only on expressing whole numbers in base 2, the place-value chart is as follows:

...	2^7	2^6	2^5	2^4	2^3	2^2	2^1	2^0

We insert a subscript "2" to the right of a number expressed in base 2. The absence of such a subscript means that the number is in base 10, by default.

For example, $110,001_2$ means:

$$110,001_2 = (1 \times 2^0) + (0 \times 2^1) + (0 \times 2^2) + (0 \times 2^3) + (1 \times 2^4) + (1 \times 2^5)$$

The corresponding base 10 number can be deciphered by expanding the right side as follows:

$$1 + 0 + 0 + 0 + 16 + 32 = 49.$$

How is a base 10 number converted to a base 2 number? The strategy is to find the largest power of 2 that divides into the given number *once*. If there is a remainder, repeat this procedure and insert zeros in the positions of the place-value chart down to the one for which that power of 2 divides into the remainder once; otherwise, fill in all positions in the place-value chart to its right with zeros.

Let's work through converting 49 to the base 2 number from the previous example:

- The largest power of 2 that divides into 49 *once* is 2^5, or 32. So, put a 1 in that position in the place-value chart and repeat the process on the remainder $49 - 32 = 17$.
- The largest power of 2 that divides into 17 *once* is 2^4, or 16. So, put a 1 in that position in the place-value chart and repeat the process on the remainder $17 - 16 = 1$.
- The largest power of 2 that divides into 1 once is 2^0, or 1. As such, put a 0 in the position in the place-value chart corresponding to 2^3, 2^2, and 2^1, and a 1 in the position corresponding to 2^0.

You were likely introduced to Roman numerals in grade school. If you have watched a movie, maybe you have paid attention to the production company screen on which the production date of the movie is listed—there, you will see a sequence of Ms, Cs, Ls, Ds, Xs, Vs, and Is. This sequence is a Roman numeral. The fact that this represents a *number* is perhaps strange since the digits are letters rather than numerals. But, each letter stands for a certain natural number:

- I = 1
- V = 5
- X = 10
- L = 50
- C = 100
- D = 500
- M = 1,000

The Roman numeral system is not a place-value system like base 2 or base 10. Rather, Roman numerals are formed by listing groups of these symbols from left to right, starting with the symbol with the largest value. To determine the base 10 number corresponding to a Roman numeral, interpret the value of each natural grouping of symbols from left to right and add them. For example, CCCXII consists of 3 hundreds, 1 ten, and 2 ones; so, its base 10 equivalent is 312.

You will never find more than three of the same symbol written consecutively in a Roman numeral. Rather, subtraction is used in the following manner:

- An I appearing directly before a V or an X means to subtract 1 from the value of that symbol. For example, IV is used instead of writing IIII to mean 4.
- An X appearing directly before an L or a C means to subtract 10 from the value of that symbol. For example, XC is used instead of LXXXX to mean 90.
- A C appearing directly before a D or an M means to subtract 100 from the value of that symbol. For example, CM is used instead of DCCCC to mean 900.

SETS AND LOGIC

Logic and sets form the foundation of mathematics. In this section, we'll review the basic terminology, symbolism, and mechanics of both.

NOTE: Around 16 percent of the questions on the DSST Math for Liberal Arts exam will test your knowledge of sets and logic.

Simple Logical Statements

A **statement** is a declarative sentence that is *either* true *or* false. It cannot be neither true nor false and it cannot be both true and false. This is known as the **Law of the Excluded Middle**.

The following are examples of statements:

- Lyndon Johnson was the 36th president of the United States.
- Andrew Wiles did not prove Fermat's Last Theorem.

An **open sentence** is any declarative sentence that contains one or more variables. An open sentence is not a statement, but becomes a statement when all the variables are assigned values.

Consider a typical example from algebra: $x - 1 = 2$. Here, x is a **variable**: it is a symbol that stands for a specific but, as of yet, unspecified real number. This sentence becomes a statement if we specify for what number x stands. The result is a true statement if x stands for 3, and a false statement if x stands for any other number.

An open sentence such as $x + 3 = 5$ or $x + y > 0$ can be made into a statement by assigning numerical values to the variable(s) x and y. But, there are other ways to convert open sentences into statements. We could ask whether there is some value of the variable for which the statement is true, or whether it is true for all possible values of the variable. This is called **quantifying** the open sentence. We do this by prefixing expressions with phrases such as "for every x," "there is an x such that," "for every x there is a y such that." The phrase "for every x" is called a **universal quantifier**. For instance, the sentence "For each real number x, $x + 3 = 5$" is a statement which happens to be false, while the statement "There is an integer x, such that $x + 3 = 5$," happens to be true.

Negation

The truth of any statement is denied by asserting the truth of its **negation**. Formally, given any statement p, the *negation of p*, denoted $\sim p$ (and read "not p"), is a statement that is true whenever p is false and false whenever p is true. For example, we deny the truth of the assertion "Today is Monday" by asserting "Today is not Monday." Equivalently, we can write the statement "It is not true that today is Monday" or "It is not the case that today is Monday." A mathematical example is: "If p is the statement '$4 + 5 < 10$,' then the negation $\sim p$ is '$4 + 5 \geq 10$.'"

Sometimes, forming the negation of a statement is more complicated. For example, consider the statement, "It rained every day this week." The negation of this statement is **not** "It did not rain every day this week." To negate this statement, it is sufficient that there be only *one* day of the week on which it did not rain. That is, the negation is, "There was a day this week on which it did not rain." The negation of the mathematical statement, "There is a real number that satisfies the equation $x^2 - 2 = 0$." is the statement, "For all real numbers x, $x^2 - 2 \neq 0$."

Compound Logical Statements and Truth Tables

Suppose we have several statements, denoted by p, q, r ... We can combine these into more complex statements by means of certain words such as *and*, *or*, *if ... then* called **logical connectives**. Since the result is a statement, it must be either true or false and its truth value depends only on the truth values of the constituent statements, not their specific content. Such statements are called **compound statements**.

The logical connective *or* is denoted by the symbol $\vee$. That is, "p or q" is denoted $p \vee q$ and is called the **disjunction** of p and q. The statement $p \vee q$ is true whenever at least one of p, q is true; it is false only when both are false. These truth values are summarized in the following **truth table**. We use T for "true" and F for "false":

p	q	$p \vee q$
T	T	T
T	F	T
F	T	T
F	F	F

For example, the disjunction "2 is even or 3 is even" is true because one of the statements is true while the other is false. The disjunction "2 is even or 3 is odd" is true because both statements are true. The disjunction, "2 is odd or 3 is even" is false because both statements are false.

The logical connective *and* is denoted by the symbol $\wedge$. That is "p and q" is denoted $p \wedge q$ and called the **conjunction** of p and q. The compound statement $p \wedge q$ is true whenever both p, q are true; it is false otherwise. These truth values are summarized as follows:

p	q	$p \wedge q$
T	T	T
T	F	T
F	T	T
F	F	F

Logically Equivalent Statements

Often, a statement can be expressed in different, yet equivalent, ways. As a simple example, consider the two statements, "Today is hot and humid." and "Today is humid and hot." If we denote the statement "Today is hot" by p and "Today is humid" by q, the first sentence is translated symbolically as $p \wedge q$, while the second is interpreted as $q \wedge p$. Clearly, if one is true so is the other, and vice versa. Such statements are said to be **logically equivalent**. More precisely, two compound statements involving one or more constituents p, q, r ... are logically equivalent provided they have the same truth value for every possible truth assignment to their constituent parts.

Some of the most important and useful logical equivalences are those concerning the negations of compound statements. Sensibly, $\sim(\sim P)$ is logically equivalent to P; this is called the **Law of the Double Negative**. In words, this is the same as saying that two "nots" in a row cancel each other.

Conditionals and Biconditionals

Another important class of mathematical assertions are those of the form "if p, then q." Statements of this form are called **conditionals** or **implications**. Such statements are denoted "$p \Rightarrow q$" and we say p *implies* q. The statement p is called the **hypothesis** and the statement q is called the **conclusion**. The commonly accepted meaning of such a statement is that the truth of p assures the truth of q. Thus, the statement would be false if we had p true and q false. However, if the conditional is to be a statement in the technical sense we defined above, it must have a truth value when p is false. The truth values are summarized as follows:

p	q	$p \Rightarrow q$
T	T	T
T	F	F
F	T	T
F	F	T

TIP: It can be shown that $p \Rightarrow q$ is equivalent to $\sim p \vee q$.

The convention that $p \Rightarrow q$ is true when p is false may seem a bit strange. To make this plausible, consider the statement, "If it rains tomorrow, then I will take you to the movies." Clearly, if it rains and I take you to the movies you will agree that I told the truth when I made the statement. Also, if it rains and I do not take you to the movies, I lied. The issue is if it does not rain, did I tell the truth or lie? In real life one might say, it does not matter. But, to be precise we are committed to assigning a truth value. And, it does not make sense to say that we *lied* in making our assertion in the case that it does not rain. So, we must have told the truth.

How do we form the negation of a conditional? Since an implication is only false when p is true and q is false, its negation is only true under those circumstances. So, the negation is only true if both p and $\sim q$ are true. But this is the same as the conjunction $p \wedge \sim q$. Thus, $\sim (p \Rightarrow q)$ is logically equivalent to the conjunction $p \wedge \sim q$.

We can form more complex statements by using more than one logical connective. For example, we could write $p \Rightarrow (q \wedge r)$. From our discussion, this statement would be true whenever p is false. It would also be true if all three statements p, q, and r are true. But, it would be false if p is true and either q or r is false (since in such case, the entire conclusion is false).

A statement of the form "p if and only if q" is called a **biconditional statement** and is denoted "$p \Leftrightarrow q$." It is true when p and q have the same truth values and is otherwise false:

....

ALERT: Constructing a truth table for such a statement is a common exam question.

....

p	q	$p \Leftrightarrow q$
T	T	T
T	F	F
F	T	F
F	F	T

By constructing a truth table, you can show that $(p \Leftrightarrow q)$ is logically equivalent to the conjunction $((p \Rightarrow q) \wedge (q \Rightarrow p))$.

De Morgan's Laws

How do we negate a disjunction or conjunction? Let us start with an example. The negation of the statement "Today is hot and humid" is "It is not true that today is hot and humid." This statement is true provided the original statement is false, and vice versa. The original statement is true if it is both hot and humid, and false if either weather condition does not hold. Therefore, the negation as written above is logically equivalent to "Today is not hot or today is not humid."

Symbolically, to negate a conjunction we proceed as follows:

Original statement: $p \wedge q$

Negation: $\sim (p \wedge q)$

Equivalent form: $\sim p \vee \sim q$

The general rule to remember here is that when you negate an "and" statement you get an "or" statement. This rule is one of **De Morgan's laws**. What about negating a disjunction? The rule is similar and results in the second of De Morgan's laws:

Original statement: $p \vee q$

Negation: $\sim (p \vee q)$

Equivalent form: $\sim p \wedge \sim q$

Contrapositive and Converse Statements

We now consider two implications related to the conditional "$p \Rightarrow q$," namely the **contrapositive** and the **converse**. Given the conditional $p \Rightarrow q$, the contrapositive is the conditional $\sim q \Rightarrow \sim p$, and the converse is the conditional $q \Rightarrow p$.

Consider the following:

Conditional: If two people share DNA, then they are related.

Contrapositive: If two people are not related, they do not share DNA.

Converse: If two people are related, then they share DNA.

All three statements are true.

Here's another, more mathematical, example:

Conditional: If triangles A and B are congruent, then they are similar.

Contrapositive: If triangles A and B are not similar, then they are not congruent.

Converse: If triangles A and B are similar, then they are congruent.

In this case, the original statement and its contrapositive are true, but the converse is not.

These examples illustrate the logical relationship among these statements. Namely, a conditional and its contrapositive are logically equivalent, but this relationship does not hold when considering the converse. That is, a conditional and its converse are not logically equivalent.

Valid Logical Arguments and Euler Diagrams

How does one prove an assertion? As we have seen, a statement of the form $p \Rightarrow q$ is true if it is impossible for p to be true and q to be false. So, we can start the proof by assuming p is, in fact, true and try to show that q must also be true. Note that if we could find a statement r such that we know—from prior knowledge or by definition—that $p \rightarrow r$ is true, then we could conclude that r must be true. If we *also* know that $r \Rightarrow q$ is true, then we could infer that q must be true. Symbolically, $[(p \Rightarrow r) \wedge (r \Rightarrow q)]$ is logically equivalent to $p \Rightarrow q$. This stringing together of implications is the main method used for constructing a valid logical argument.

The following **syllogism** (two statements or premises followed by a conclusion) illustrates this method:

All soft things are comfortable.

All blankets are soft.

Thus, all blankets are comfortable.

We say the syllogism is **valid** if whenever the structure of the syllogism means that if the premises are true then the conclusion cannot be false. Validity relates to logical structure. But not all valid arguments are sound. If someone found a blanket that was not soft, then this argument would be unsound as one of the premises would be false.

A pictorial way of determining if a syllogism is valid is by using an **Euler diagram**. Let's construct one for the above example. Here, we have two sets of objects: "Blankets" and "Things that are soft." Sensibly, the first set is entirely included within the second, a fact that we illustrate as follows:

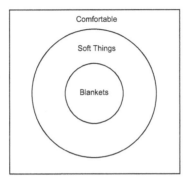

Consider our syllogism from earlier, now with some added premises:

All soft things are comfortable.

All blankets are soft.

The wool jacket is not comfortable.

Thus, the wool jacket is not a blanket.

Sometimes, it is difficult to parse the relationship among premises without using a diagram. This time, we have the same two sets, but we additionally have an object that does not belong to the set "Things that are soft." As such, the Euler diagram for this syllogism is as follows:

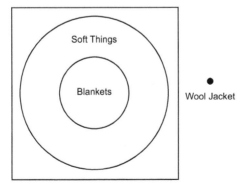

From this diagram, the object "wool jacket" does not belong to the set "blankets," so the conclusion is true. Hence, the syllogism is valid.

The Nature of Sets and Set-Builder Notation

Let's informally think of a **set** as a collection of objects. The objects that make up a set can be numbers, words, shapes, sets, or other symbols that are referred to as **elements** (or *members*) of the set. Sets are usually labeled using uppercase Latin letters (e.g., A, B, C) and the elements of a given set by lowercase Latin letters (e.g., a, b, c).

Some sets can be displayed by explicitly listing all of its members and enclosing this list of elements within braces { }. For example, if A denotes the set whose members are 1, 2, and 3, we would write $A = \{1, 2, 3\}$. When the number of members of a set becomes rather large, it can be cumbersome (or even impossible) to list all of them explicitly. In such case we need an alternate way, commonly referred to as **set-builder notation**, to describe the set. Precisely, if $P(x)$ is an open sentence and if A is the set of all those objects satisfying $P(x)$, then we write $A = \{x : P(x)\}$, or equivalently $A = \{x\ P(x)\}$, and read this is "A is the set of all x such that $P(x)$ is true."

Consider the following examples:

- Let $P(x)$ be the open sentence, "x is a positive integer less than 21 and x is divisible by 5." Observe that 5, 10, 15, and 20 are the only elements of the set $A = \{x : P(x)\}$. Since the number of elements is small, it is more convenient to write $A = \{5, 10, 15, 20\}$.
- Let $P(x)$ be the open sentence, "x is an integer and x is a multiple of 3." If $C = \{x : P(x)\}$ then, $C = \{x : \text{There exists an integer } k \text{ such that } x = 3k\}$. Equivalently, $C = \{0, \pm 3, \pm 6, \dots\}$.

Set Membership and Containment

All elements under consideration in a discussion must come from *some* tacitly understood **universal set** U—this is an underlying set that contains all possible elements that any of our sets in the discussion can ever contain.

A set that has no members is called the **empty set** and is denoted by $\emptyset$. If A is a nonempty set and x is an element of A, we denote this fact by writing $x \in A$, read as, "x is an element of A."

We use this notion of **membership** to give meaning to a **containment** relationship that sometimes exists between two sets. Precisely, let A and B be two sets. We say that A is a **subset** of B and write $A \subseteq B$ if $x \in A \Rightarrow x \in B$. A standard way of illustrating such containment is by drawing a so-called **Venn diagram** (which resembles an Euler diagram), as shown in the following:

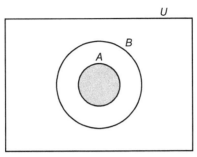

If $A \subseteq B$ and $B \subseteq A$, then we say A is *equal* to B, denoted by $A = B$. If $A \subseteq B$ and $A \neq B$, then A is called a **proper subset** of B, or $A \subset B$.

Set Operations

Just as several different arithmetic operations can be performed on real numbers, there are also operations, listed below, that can be performed on sets to produce another set.

Set Operation	Set (in symbols)	Set (in words)	Venn Diagram
Complement A^c	$\left\{ \begin{array}{l} x: x \in U \\ \text{and } x \notin A \end{array} \right\}$	All members of the universal set that are not in A.	
Union $A \cup B$	$\left\{ \begin{array}{l} x \in U: x \in A \\ \text{or } x \in B \end{array} \right\}$	All members of the universal set that are in A, B, or both.	
Intersection $A \cap B$	$\left\{ \begin{array}{l} x \in U: x \in A \\ \text{and } x \in B \end{array} \right\}$	All members of the universal set that are in both A and B.	

If $A \cap B = \emptyset$, then A and B are said to be **disjointed**.

Interpreting Venn Diagrams

Venn diagrams are useful aids when visualizing complicated relationships. A single diagram can contain a lot of information about how various sets are related. For instance, consider the Venn diagram shown here:

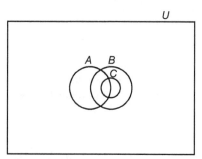

The following statements can be made concerning sets A, B, and C, and their elements:

- Every element of C belongs to B.
- Some elements of B are in A.
- Not every member of C is in A and B.
- If an object is not in B, then it cannot be in C.

If the sets A, B, and C are described in context, then these mathematical statements also take on contextual meaning. Suppose we take as the universal set the set of all senior students in High School X, and that we impose the following context on sets A, B, and C:

- A is the set of all students who play sports.
- B is the set of all students who plan to attend college next year.
- C is the set of all students taking AP classes.

Then, the mathematical statement, "Every element of C belongs to B" is interpreted as "Every student taking AP classes intends to attend college next year." Likewise, the mathematical statement "Not every member of C is in A and B" is interpreted as "Not every student taking AP classes both plays sports and plans to attend college next year."

METRIC SYSTEM, CONVERSIONS, AND GEOMETRY

On the DSST exam, you will need to be familiar with basic conversions involving the US customary unit system and metric system, as well as mathematical and applied problems involving elementary geometry. This section will review the major concepts you should know before test day.

> **NOTE:** Approximately 12 percent of the questions on the DSST Math for Liberal Arts exam cover the metric system, conversions, and geometry.

US Customary Unit System and Metric System

Different units of measurement are used to quantify different types of quantities, like time, speed, liquid measures, length, area, and volume. Below are some common units of measure expressed in equivalent ways.

Type of quantity being measured	Units of measure and their conversions
Time	1 minute = 60 seconds 1 hour = 60 minutes = 3,600 seconds 1 day = 24 hours = 1,440 minutes = 86,400 seconds
Weight	1 pound = 16 ounces 1 ton = 2,000 pounds
Liquid Measure	1 gallon = 4 quarts = 8 pints = 16 cups 1 quart = 2 pints = 4 cups 1 pint = 2 cups
Length	1 foot = 12 inches 1 yard = 3 feet = 36 inches 1 mile = 1,760 yards = 5,280 feet
Area	1 square foot = $(12 \text{ inches})^2 = 12^2$ square inches 1 square yard = $(3 \text{ feet})^2 = 3^2$ square feet 1 square mile = $(5,280 \text{ feet})^2 = 5,280^2$ square feet
Volume	1 cubic foot = $(12 \text{ inches})^3 = 12^3$ cubic inches 1 cubic yard = $(3 \text{ feet})^3 = 3^3$ cubic feet

> **NOTE:** The abbreviated notation ft.^{2} means *square feet* and ft.^{3} means *cubic feet*. The same exponentiation notation is used for all units.

The **metric system** is based on powers of 10 and applies to units of length, area, volume, and liquid measure. The basic unit of length measure is the *meter* (m). This unit is squared and cubed to get the units of measure for area and volume, respectively; the unit names are *square meters* (m^2) and *cubic meters* (m^3). The unit used for measuring volumes of liquid is the *liter* (L), which is defined by $1 L = 1 dm^3$, and the unit used for measuring weight is the *gram* (g). The following is a list of commonly used prefixes and their associated powers of 10:

Prefix	Abbreviation	Power of 10
mega	M	10^6
kilos	k	10^3
hecto	h	10^2
deca	da	10^1
---	*base unit*	10^0
deci	d	10^{-1}
centi	c	10^{-2}
milli	m	10^{-3}
micro	μ	10^{-6}

Unit Conversions

Knowing how to convert from one unit to another is important when trying to solve problems in which similar quantities are expressed using different units.

Let's start with the metric system. Since the metric system is based on powers of 10, converting units expressed in the metric system is simply a matter of appropriately moving the decimal point. For example, 300 cm = 3 m because $1 cm = 10^{-2}$ m; therefore, multiplying both sides by 300 yields the result. Likewise, 400 dm = 40 m since $1 dm = 10^{-1}$ m. In both cases, note that the conversion simply involved moving the decimal point to the *left* the number of places indicated by the power without the negative sign (2 and 1, respectively). This is always true when converting a unit lower on the table to one higher up. The exact opposite is true if you are converting a unit higher on the table to one lower. For instance, 2 km = 200 hm because 1 km = 100 hm.

Performing conversions of units of area or volume also are simple matters of moving the decimal point. But the number of places the decimal point is moved for area conversions is now double what it was for length conversions, and triple for volume conversions. The reason is that the units themselves are squared and cubed to get units of area and volume measure, respectively. For instance, since 1 cm = 10^{-2} m, it follows that 1 cm^2 = (1 cm)^2 = (10 and cubed to get units of area and volume measure, respectively. For instance, since 1 cm = 10^{-2} m)^2 = 10^{-4} m^2. To convert from square centimeters to square meters, the decimal point must be moved to the left *four* units, not two as it was for length measure. The same reasoning works for volume unit conversions.

TIP: In the metric system, when converting from a smaller unit to a larger unit, move the decimal point to the left the appropriate number of places; when converting from a larger to a smaller unit, move it to the right.

Converting units in the US customary system is slightly more involved only because the units are not based on powers of 10. Here, the key is to set up products of fractions that show the original units canceling and the new units remaining in the final product. For example, to convert 3.5 feet to inches, we use the conversion factor 1 foot = 12 inches in the following computation:

$$3.5 \text{ feet} = \frac{3.5 \text{ feet}}{1} \times \frac{12 \text{ inches}}{1 \text{ foot}} = \frac{3.5 \text{ feet}}{1} \times \frac{12 \text{ inches}}{1 \text{ foot}} = (3.5) \cdot (12) \text{ inches} = 42 \text{ inches}$$

This works because the fraction $\dfrac{12 \text{ inches}}{1 \text{ foot}} = 1$.

Converting units of speed involves making *two* conversions—one for the numerator and one for the denominator. For example, to convert 85 miles per hour to *feet per minute*, we use the conversion factors 1 mile = 5,280 feet and 1 hour = 60 minutes and perform the following computation:

$$\frac{85 \text{ miles}}{1 \text{ hour}} = \frac{85 \text{ miles}}{1 \text{ hour}} \times \frac{5,280 \text{ feet}}{1 \text{ mile}} \times \frac{1 \text{ hour}}{60 \text{ minutes}} = \frac{85 \times 5,280}{60} \text{ feet per minute}$$

You can also convert between the metric and US customary systems, but you need to use established conversion factors (like 1 m ≈ 3.28 feet) to do so. In such case, you would be given the necessary conversion factors on the exam.

Basic Notions in Geometry

You have encountered the terms *point, line, line segment, ray,* and *angle* throughout your education. We will focus on the terminology that is likely less familiar in this short section.

Angles are classified according to their "size" measured using **degrees**. The notation m∠A is used to denote the measure of angle A. The following is some basic angle terminology:

Term	Definition
Acute Angle	An angle with measure between 0 and 90 degrees.
Right Angle	An angle with measure of 90 degrees.
Obtuse Angle	An angle with measure between 90 and 180 degrees.
Complementary Angles	Two angles with measures that sum to 90 degrees.
Supplementary Angles	Two angles with measures that sum to 180 degrees.
Congruent Angles	Two angles with the same measure.

The relationships between pairs of angles are also important to recognize. We've identified these relationships in the following diagram that shows two parallel lines intersected by a transversal.

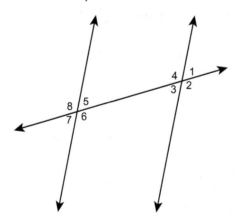

Term	Examples from Diagram
Vertical Angles	∠1 and ∠3; ∠2 and ∠4; ∠5 and ∠7; ∠6 and ∠8
Adjacent Angles	∠1 and ∠2; ∠3 and ∠4; ∠5 and ∠6; ∠7 and ∠8
Corresponding Angles	∠1 and ∠5; ∠2 and ∠6; ∠3 and ∠7; ∠4 and ∠8
Alternate Interior Angles	∠4 and ∠6; ∠3 and ∠5
Alternate Exterior Angles	∠2 and ∠8; ∠1 and ∠7

Triangles and Quadrilaterals

Two important rules that all triangles obey are the Triangle Sum Rule and Triangle Inequality. The **Triangle Sum Rule** says that the sum of the measures of the three angles in any triangle must be 180°. **Triangle Inequality** says that the sum of the lengths of any two sides of a triangle must be strictly larger than the length of the third side. It is impossible to construct a triangle that does not satisfy *both* conditions.

The **Pythagorean theorem** relates the lengths of the sides of *right* triangles. For the right triangle shown below, the sides with lengths a and b are called legs and the side opposite the right angle is the **hypotenuse**; the hypotenuse is the longest side of a right triangle. The Pythagorean theorem says that $a^2 + b^2 = c^2$.

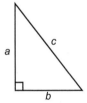

TIP: The Pythagorean theorem ONLY works for right triangles!

Quadrilaterals are figures in the plane with four sides, each of which is a line segment. There are several common quadrilaterals (e.g., square, rectangle, parallelogram) that arise in solving practical problems.

Perimeter and Area of Planar Regions

The **perimeter** of a region in the plane is the "distance around." The **area** of a region in the plane is the number of *unit squares* needed to cover the shape. The following are some standard perimeter and area formulas with which you should be familiar.

Region	Illustration	Perimeter Formula	Area Formula
Square		$P = 4s$	$A = s^2$
Rectangle		$P = 2l + 2w$	$A = l \times w$
Circle		The perimeter of a circle is called the circumference; it's found with two common expressions: $P = 2\pi r = \pi d$	$A = \pi r^2$
Arc of Circle		$P = \left(\dfrac{\theta}{360°}\right) \cdot \pi 2r$	$A = \left(\dfrac{\theta}{360°}\right) \cdot \pi r^2$
Triangle		Sum the three lengths of the triangle.	$A = \dfrac{1}{2}b \cdot h$

TIP: Do NOT include *h* in the perimeter of a triangle unless it is an actual leg of the triangle.

Questions involving perimeter and area will be somewhat more complicated than merely applying these formulas. In fact, questions often involve concepts from multiple categories. For instance, you might be asked to determine a formula for the area of a new rectangle formed by reducing the width and length of a different rectangle by a certain percentage. In such case, you need to know about area formulas and how to work with percentages.

Other common questions will ask you to compute the perimeter or area of a geometric figure that is comprised of smaller, identifiable shapes, such as the following:

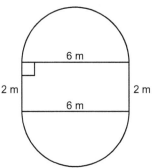

This figure is composed of two congruent semicircles whose radii are 3 m (since the diameter is 6 m) and a rectangle. The area of each semicircle is $\frac{1}{2}\pi(3m)^2 = \frac{9}{2}\pi\,m^2$ and the area of the rectangle is $(2\text{ m})(6\text{ m}) = 12\text{ m}^2$. So, the area enclosed by the figure is $2\left(\frac{9}{2}\pi\,m^2\right) + 12\text{ m}^2 = (9\pi + 12)\text{m}^2$.

For the perimeter, do NOT include the sides with lengths 6 m since they are inside the figure. The perimeter is the distance *around* the figure! The lengths of the two semicircles and two short sides of the rectangle are all that are used. The length of each semicircle is $\frac{1}{2}\left(2\pi \bullet 3\text{m}\right) = 3\pi\,\text{m}$. The perimeter is $3\pi\text{ m} + 3\pi\text{ m} + 2(2\text{ m}) = (6\pi + 4)\text{ m}$.

Surface Area and Volume of Solids

Two measures of interest for three-dimensional solids are **surface area** and **volume**. Conceptually, to compute the surface area of a solid, the solid is dissected and flattened out so that it can be visualized as a combination of recognizable figures whose areas can be computed using known formulas. The volume of a solid in space is the number of *unit cubes* needed to fill it. The following are formulas for the surface area and volume of some common solids:

Solid	Illustration	Surface Area Formula	Volume Formula
Cube		$SA = 6e^2$	$V = e^3$
Rectangular Prism		$SA = 2(lw + lh + wh)$	$V = lwh$

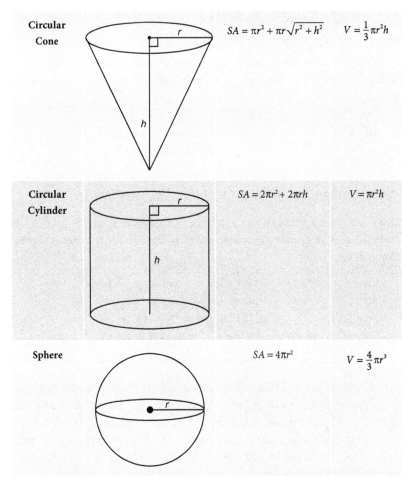

Circular Cone	$SA = \pi r^2 + \pi r \sqrt{r^2 + h^2}$	$V = \frac{1}{3}\pi r^2 h$
Circular Cylinder	$SA = 2\pi r^2 + 2\pi r h$	$V = \pi r^2 h$
Sphere	$SA = 4\pi r^2$	$V = \frac{4}{3}\pi r^3$

As with problems concerning the area of planar regions, common questions concerning volume and surface area will involve decomposing a more complicated solid into smaller solids whose surface area and volume are easily computed using known formulas. Other types of problems will involve a crossover to algebra. For example, if a spherical balloon has surface area 36π square centimeters, what is its volume? Determining the volume of a sphere requires that you have the radius, and this information is readily attainable from the surface area formula. Indeed, solving the equation $4\pi r^2 = 36\pi$ for r yields $r = 3$ cm. As such, the volume of the sphere is

$$\frac{4}{3}\pi(3 \text{ cm})^3 = \frac{4}{3}\pi \cdot 27 = 36\pi \text{ cm}^3.$$

ALGEBRA, GRAPHS, AND FUNCTIONS

The subject of algebra is vast. The DSST exam focuses deeply on a handful of the topics rather than requiring you to know every nuance and every technique. The following section will highlight the important topics you need to know.

> **NOTE:** Around 11 percent of the questions on the DSST Math for Liberal Arts exam test your knowledge of algebra, graphs, and functions.

Order of Operations and Algebraic Expressions

Often, you need to simplify an arithmetic expression involving all types of real numbers and operations. You must use the following **order of operations** rules:

- **Step 1:** Simplify all expressions contained within parentheses.
- **Step 2:** Simplify all expressions involving exponents.
- **Step 3:** Perform all multiplication and division as it arises from left to right.
- **Step 4:** Perform all addition and subtraction as it arises from left to right.

If there are multiple groupings, apply the same steps *within* each grouping.

When evaluating algebraic expressions for specific values of the variables, simply substitute the values in for the variables and simplify the resulting arithmetic expression using the arithmetic rules involving integers, fractions, and decimals, together with the order of operations. For example, to evaluate the algebraic expression $1 - x^3(2x - y^2)$ when $x = -2$ and $y = 3$, substitute these values into the expression and simplify:

$$1 - (-2)^3\left(2(-2) - (3)^2\right) = 1 - (-2)^3(-4\ -9)$$
$$= 1 - (-2)^3(-13)$$
$$= 1 - (-8)(-13)$$
$$= 1 - 104$$
$$= -103$$

Evaluating and Manipulating Formulas

Formulas relating two or more quantities arise in nearly all fields of study and in everyday life. Whether it's converting degrees Fahrenheit to degrees

Celsius using the formula $C = \dfrac{5}{9}(F - 32)$ or determining the height of a baseball struck at a certain height above home plate with a certain speed using the well-known physics formula $s = \dfrac{1}{2}gt^2 + v_0 t + s_0$, you have likely encountered *some* formula for *some* reason. You will need to manipulate and evaluate formulas on the DSST exam. Typically, a description of the context of a formula will be given and you will be asked to determine the value of one of the variables given the values of the others.

For instance, suppose the temperature of a computer lab is 12 degrees Celsius and you're asked to determine the temperature in degrees Fahrenheit. This requires substituting $C = 12$ into $C = \dfrac{5}{9}(F - 32)$ and solving for F:

$$C = \frac{5}{9}(F - 32)$$

$$12 = \frac{5}{9}(F - 32)$$

$$12 \cdot \frac{9}{5} = F - 32$$

$$12 \cdot \frac{9}{5} + 32 = F$$

$$53.6 = F$$

Sometimes, rather than being given values for the other variables, you will be asked to solve a formula for a specific variable. This sort of algebraic manipulation uses the properties of fractions and integers, the order of operations, and the notion of **balancing an equation**. For example, you might be asked to solve the area formula for a trapezoid $A = \dfrac{1}{2}h(a + b)$, where the bases have lengths a and b and the height is h, for b. There are two ways to proceed which yield different looking, yet equivalent, results:

$$A = \frac{1}{2}h(a + b) \qquad\qquad A = \frac{1}{2}h(a + b)$$

$$2A = h(a + b) \qquad\qquad 2A = h(a + b)$$

$$2A = ha + hb \qquad\qquad \frac{2A}{h} = a + b$$

$$2A - ha = hb \qquad\qquad \frac{2A}{h} - a = b$$

$$\frac{2A - ha}{h} = b$$

Applications of Linear Equations

Setting up linear equations to solve applied problems is an important skill to master. Many word problems will require you to use linear equations—some examples might ask about rates, mixtures, time, cost, or work. The following is a sampling of these problems, along with a discussion of how to best set up the linear equation to solve them.

Problem: Tom scored 12, 7, 5, and 6 goals in each of his first four hockey games at a weekend tournament. How many goals does he need in the fifth game so that his average is 8 goals per game for the first five games?

Set-up: Let x be the number of goals scored in the fifth game. The average number of goals for 5 games is computed by summing the goals scored in the five games and dividing the sum by 5. Since this average is supposed to be 8, we arrive at this equation:

$$\frac{12+7+5+6+x}{5} = 8$$
$$12+7+5+6+x = 40$$
$$30+x = 40$$
$$x = 10$$

Tom must score 10 goals in his fifth game for an average of 8 goals per game.

Problem: The Eagle Coffee and Tea Company makes a tea blend of chai tea worth $2.50 per kilogram and Darjeeling worth $2.00 per kilogram. How many kilograms of each should be used to produce a 20-kilogram tea blend with a total value of $46.00?

Set-up: Let x be the number of kilograms of chai tea used. Then, there are $(20 - x)$ kilograms of Darjeeling tea used. Multiply each by the corresponding cost per kilogram, sum the two costs, and set the sum equal to $46 to get the equation:

$$2.50x + 2.00(20 - x) = 46$$
$$2.5x + 40 - 2x = 46$$
$$0.5x = 6$$
$$x = 12$$

So the company uses 12 kilograms of chai tea and 8 kilograms of Darjeeling tea.

Problem: A 10% salt solution is to be mixed with a 20% salt solution to obtain 100 gallons of an 18% salt solution. How many gallons of each original solution should be used to form the mixture?

Set-up: Let x be the number of gallons of 10% salt solution. Then, there are $(100 - x)$ gallons of 20% salt solution. Multiply each by the corresponding concentration—doing so gives the amount of salt in each of these two mixtures. Sum these quantities and set the sum equal to the amount of salt in 100 gallons of 18% solution to get the equation:

$$0.10x + 0.20(100 - x) = 0.18(100)$$
$$0.10x + 20 - 0.20x = 18$$
$$-0.10x = -2$$
$$x = 20$$

So the final answer is 10 gallons of 10% salt solution and 90 gallons of 20% salt solution.

Problem: A train traveled from Newark to St. Louis in 20 hours. It returned from St. Louis to Newark along the same route in 15 hours since its average speed was 25 miles per hour faster on the return trip. Find the distance from Newark to St. Louis.

Set-up: Let x be the rate (in mph) of the trip from Newark to St. Louis. Then, the rate of the reverse trip is $(x + 25)$ mph. Using distance = rate × time, an expression for the distance of the Newark to St. Louis trip is $20x$ and an expression for the distance traveled for the reverse trip is $15(x + 25)$. Since the same route is used, the distances traveled for both trips are the same. Equate these expressions to get the equation:

$$20x = 15(x + 25)$$
$$20x = 15x + 375$$
$$5x = 375$$
$$x = 75$$

Now that we know the rate of the trip from Newark to St. Louis (75 miles per hour), and the time (20 hours), we can find the distance. Let d be the distance from Newark to St. Louis. Using the formula distance = rate × time, solve as follows:

$$d = 20 \times 75 = 1,500$$

Ratios and Proportions

A **ratio** is a comparison of one positive quantity x to another positive quantity y expressed as a fraction $\frac{x}{y}$ or using the notation $x{:}y$ (read "x to y"). For instance, if there are 4 girls to every 3 boys in a class, we say that the ratio of girls to boys is 4:3, or 4 to 3. The order in which a ratio is expressed is important because of the representation as a fraction. We could alternatively describe the above example using the ratio "3 boys for every 4 girls" and say the ratio of boys to girls is 3:4—this conveys the same information. However, since $\frac{3}{4} \neq \frac{4}{3}$, the two ratios are not equal.

A **proportion** is an equation relating two ratios; it is expressed by equating two fractions, say $\frac{a}{b} = \frac{c}{d}$. Proportions are formulated when one ratio is known and one of the two quantities in an equivalent ratio is unknown. They arise when changing units of measure and similar triangles, just to name a couple.

Let's look at a sample problem.

> **Problem:** Suppose there are 2 hockey sticks for every 5 pucks in the storage locker room. If the last count was 60 pucks, how many hockey sticks are in the storage room?
>
> **Set-up:** Let h denote the number of hockey sticks in the storage room. Set up the proportion:
>
> $$\frac{2}{5} = \frac{h}{60}$$
> $$5h = 120$$
> $$h = 24$$

Applications Involving Graphs of Equations in Two Variables

The **graph of an equation of two variables** is the collection of all ordered pairs (x,y) in the xy-coordinate plane that satisfy the equation—that is, when the respective values for x and y are substituted into the equation, the result is a true statement. You should be able to interpret a graph in a context and use it to answer questions in that context.

Consider the following scenario.

A tool salesperson earns $42,000 as an annual base salary and earns commission as indicated in the following graph:

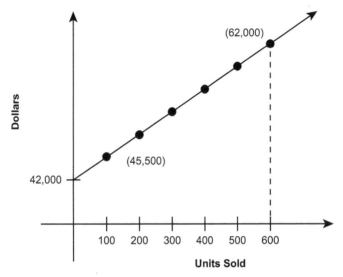

You might be asked how many units the salesperson must sell to earn an annual salary of $62,000. From the graph, it is evident he or she must sell 600 tools.

The graph might not be linear in nature, but you should be able to interpret parts of the graph in context and extract information. For instance, the following graph represents the height of a rock above the ground after it has been thrown by a hiker.

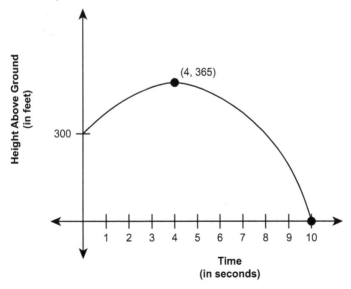

It is evident from the graph that the rock was thrown starting at a height of 300 feet above the ground, that the maximum height above the ground the rock achieves is 365 feet, and that it traveled for 10 seconds before hitting the ground. You will likely have to interpret graphs like these for questions on the DSST exam.

Elementary Functions

Physicists, biologists, economists, and others often have the need to relate one variable to another in their work. Typical questions testing these skills might look like these:

- How is the pressure in an inner tube related to the thickness of the tubing?
- How is weight related to the effectiveness of an allergy medication?
- How does projected profit depend on the number of units sold to early-adopters?

The notion relating one quantity to another is described mathematically by a **function**. A function f is a rule that assigns to each element x in one set A exactly one element y, denoted $f(x)$, in another set B. When working with functions, we need to compute the **functional value** $f(x)$ for different inputs. For instance, if we want to compute the functional value when $x = -2$ for the function $f(x) = x^3 + 2x - 5$, we would simply plug in -2 for x:

$$f(-2) = (-2)^3 + 2(-2) - 5 = -8 - 4 - 5 = -17$$

You may be asked to perform such a computation for any number of functions, including those with an expression involving multiple powers, the square root, or absolute value of the input. In all cases, the way you compute the functional value is the same: substitute the given value in for the variable and simplify the resulting arithmetic expression using the rules of arithmetic. The set of points that you *can* plug in for the input is called the **domain**. For example, for the function $f(x) = \sqrt{1 - x}$, you can substitute any value of x for which $1 - x \geq 0$. But, any value of x for which $1 - x < 0$ would result in a negative radicand, which yields a meaningless output.

The graph of a function is the set of points in the xy-plane of the form $(x, f(x))$, where x belongs to the domain of the function f. An x-value belongs to the domain of f if an ordered pair with that x-value is part of the graph of f.

But not all graphs represent functions. If you have a graph of a relationship, an easy way to determine if it defines a function is to apply the so-called **vertical line test**. To do so, determine if any vertical line that intersects the graph in *more than one* point. If the answer is "yes," then the relationship is NOT a function; otherwise, it is a function.

Graphs can possess various characteristics, all of which have specific meanings when the function is described in a context. For one, a function $f(x)$ equals zero whenever its graph touches the x-axis. If the graph of $y = f(x)$ is *above* the x-axis for all values of x between real numbers a and b, then the corresponding y-values at these x-values are positive. In such case, we say the function is **positive** on this set of x-values. Likewise, if the graph of $y = f(x)$ is *below* the x-axis on this set of x-values, the function is said to be **negative** on this set.

Next, as you move from left to right throughout a portion of the x-axis and you inspect the shape of the graph of a function, one of three things must happen:

- The graph climbs upward.
- The graph declines downward.
- Or the points remain on the same horizontal line.

A function is said to be **increasing** if the graph climbs upward from left to right, and **decreasing** if the graph declines downward from left to right. A function is **constant** if the points lie on a horizontal line.

For example, the **value function** (that is, how much the company is worth if it were to be purchased) for a new upstart financial consultation company is graphed below:

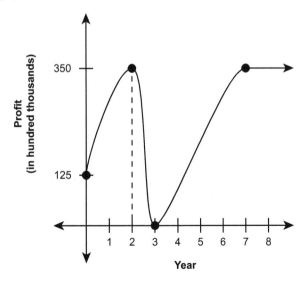

Some contextual observations are as follows:

- The value of the company increased considerably during the first two years, but then fell precipitously the next year until it was worthless. Thereafter, its value increased during the next 4 years and leveled off.
- The maximum worth of the company is $35,000,000.

LINEAR SYSTEMS AND INEQUALITIES

As a continuation of the previous section, let's now delve a bit deeper and focus on graphing and solving linear equations and systems of linear equations and inequalities.

> **NOTE:** Around 8 percent of the questions on the DSST Math for Liberal Arts exam test your knowledge of linear systems and inequalities.

Graphs of Linear Equations

First, we'll explore the graphs of linear functions in detail. A key concept to understand is that associated with every line is a **slope**. Suppose two points (x_1, y_1) and (x_2, y_2), with $x_1 \neq x_2$, lie on a line. The **slope**, m, of the line is defined as $m = \dfrac{y_2 - y_1}{x_2 - x_1}$. This number is an indication of the steepness of the line. A negative number means the line slants downward as the x-values increase from left to right, whereas a positive number means the line slants upward from left to right. The larger the absolute value of the number, the steeper the line.

The equation of a line can be written in one of three forms. The most common is the **slope-intercept** form $y = mx + b$, where m is the slope of the line and b is the y-coordinate of its y-intercept. The latter is true because the y-intercept of an equation's graph occurs when $x = 0$.

> **TIP:** If you have one point and a slope, or if you have two points, you can write the equation of a line!

There are a variety of questions concerning lines, within and outside of a context, that can be asked on the DSST exam. Here are some common scenarios:

- Find the equation of a line given two points—they can be written or part of a graph.
- Find the equation of a line passing through a given point that is either parallel or perpendicular to a different line. (Two lines are **parallel** if they have the same slope; two lines are **perpendicular** if the product of their slopes is −1.)
- Find rate of change of a quantity y with respect to x if the relationship is linear and given by a graph.

For example, suppose you are asked to find the equation of the line that has slope $m = 2$ and that passes through the point $(3,10)$. What would you do? Well, since we want $(3,10)$ to lie on the line, we can use any other point (x,y), which is also on the line, and use the slope formula to deduce that $\dfrac{y-10}{x-3} = 2$. Solve for y:

$$\frac{y-10}{x-3} = 2$$
$$(x-3)\frac{y-10}{x-3} = 2(x-3)$$
$$y-10 = 2(x-3)$$
$$y-10 = 2x-6$$
$$y = 2x+4$$

Solving Linear Equations

Solving linear equations involves simplifying various expressions using the order of operations, together with the distributive property of multiplication, to isolate the variable on one side of the equation. You must balance both sides of the equations. The same basic strategy is also used to solve linear inequalities, with one additional feature: the inequality sign is switched whenever both sides of the inequality are multiplied or divided by a negative real number. Also, the **solution set** of an inequality (that is, the set of real numbers that satisfies the inequality) contains infinitely many values, whereas a linear equation has *one* solution.

Consider the following:

$$\frac{\frac{1}{2}x-4}{3} = \frac{x+8}{5}$$

$$15 \cdot \left(\frac{\frac{1}{2}x-4}{3}\right) = 15 \cdot \frac{x+8}{5}$$

$$5 \cdot \left(\frac{1}{2}x-4\right) = 3(x+8)$$

$$\frac{5}{2}x-20 = 3x+24$$

$$2 \cdot \left(\frac{5}{2}x-20\right) = 2 \cdot 3x+24$$

$$5x-40 = 6x+48$$

$$5x-88 = 6x$$

$$-88 = x$$

$$\frac{\frac{1}{2}x-4}{3} < \frac{x+8}{5}$$

$$15 \cdot \left(\frac{\frac{1}{2}x-4}{3}\right) < 15 \cdot \frac{x+8}{5}$$

$$5 \cdot \left(\frac{1}{2}x-4\right) < 3(x+8)$$

$$\frac{5}{2}x-20 < 3x+24$$

$$2 \cdot \left(\frac{5}{2}x-20\right) < 2 \cdot 3x+24$$

$$5x-40 < 6x+48$$

$$5x-88 < 6x$$

$$-88 < x$$

Systems of Linear Equations

Two or more equations considered simultaneously form a **system** of equations. Consider the system:

$$\begin{cases} 3x-2y=2 \\ x+2y=-2 \end{cases}$$

Since the point $(0, -1)$ satisfies both equations in the system, we say that $(0, -1)$ is a **solution** of the system. On the other hand, the ordered pair $(2,2)$ is NOT a solution of the given system because it does not satisfy BOTH equations.

There are three methods for solving such systems: elimination, substitution, and graphing.

Elimination	Substitution	Graphing
Strategy: Multiply one or both equations, if needed, by appropriate numbers so that upon doing so and adding the equations results in one variable being canceled. Solve for the other variable, and then plug it back into either equation to find the value of the second variable.	**Strategy:** Solve one of the equations for a variable. Substitute this expression for that same variable in the other equation. This yields a linear equation in one variable. Solve it. Then, plug the solution into the expression used for substitution to find the value of the second variable.	**Strategy:** Put each equation in slope-intercept form and graph them. There are three possibilities: • There is one intersection point that is the solution of the system. • There are NO intersection points, so the lines are **parallel**. There is no solution in this case. • The lines are identical. In such case, every point on the line is a solution of the system.
Solution: $\begin{cases} 3x - 2y = 2 \\ x + 2y = -2 \end{cases}$ Add the equations to get $4x = 0$. So, $x = 0$. Now, substitute this back into either equation, say the first one, to get $3(0) - 2y = 2$. So, $y = -1$. Thus, the solution of the system is $(0, -1)$.	**Solution:** $\begin{cases} 3x - 2y = 2 \\ x + 2y = -2 \end{cases}$ Solve the second equation for x: $x = -2 - 2y$. Substitute this expression into the first equation: $3(-2 - 2y) - 2y = 2$ Solve for y: $-6 - 6y - 2y = 2$ $\qquad -8y = 8$ $\qquad\quad y = -1$ Plug this into $x = -2 - 2y$ to see that $x = 0$. Thus, the solution of the system is $(0, -1)$.	**Solution:** $\begin{cases} 3x - 2y = 2 \\ x + 2y = -2 \end{cases}$ The equations are: $y = \dfrac{3}{2}x - 1,\ y = -\dfrac{1}{2}x - 1$ The graphs are the lines as follows: 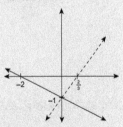 The intersection point is $(0, -1)$, which is the solution of the system.

Systems of linear equations are used to solve real-world problems like those modeled using single linear equations. Let's walk through how to set up several such problems.

Problem: Tickets to a production of *The Color Purple* at a local university cost $6 for general admission or $3 with a student I.D. If 225 people paid to see a performance and $1,071 was collected, how many of each type of admission were sold?

Set-up: Let x be the number of general admission tickets sold and y the number of student tickets sold. Create two linear equations involving x and y. First, since there are 225 tickets sold all told, we know that $x + y = 225$. Next, multiply the number of each type of ticket by its price, sum the two dollar amounts, and equate it to the total collected, $1,071. Doing so yields the second equation $6x + 3y = 1,071$. So, the system is as follows:

$$\begin{cases} x + y = 225 \\ 6x + 3y = 1{,}071 \end{cases}$$

Problem: Traveling for 3 hours into a steady head wind, a plane makes a trip of 1,450 miles. The pilot determines that flying with the same wind for 2 hours, she could make a trip of 1,150 miles. What is the speed of the plane in the absence of wind and what is the speed of the wind?

Set-up: Let x be the speed of the plane in the absence of wind and y be the speed of the wind. A head wind reduces the plane's speed, while a tail wind (or traveling *with* the wind) increases the plane's speed. Using distance equals rate *times* time, the equation for the trip *into* the wind is $1,450 = 3(x - y)$ and the equation for the trip *with* the wind is $1,150 = 2(x + y)$. So, the system is

$$\begin{cases} 1{,}450 = 3(x - y) \\ 1{,}150 = 2(x + y) \end{cases}$$

Linear Inequalities in Two Variables

Just as the nature of the solution set for a linear equation in one variable differed from the nature of the solution set of a linear inequality in one variable—a linear equation has one solution while a linear inequality has infinitely many solutions—the nature of the set of points that satisfy a linear equation in two variables is different from the solution set of a linear inequality in two variables.

To determine the solution set of a linear inequality in two variables, start by graphing the line. If the inequality symbol is < or >, the boundary line will be dotted; if the inequality symbol is ≤ or ≥, the boundary line will be solid. Then, the only extra step is to choose a point either above or below the line and see if it satisfies the inequality. If it does, then shade the entire region containing that point on that side of the line; otherwise, shade the entire region on the other side of the line.

Consider the following examples:

Sketch the Solution Set of $y + x > 4$	Sketch the Solution Set of $y + x \le 4$
Graph the related linear equation $y + x = 4$. The slope-intercept form is $y = -x + 4$. The slope is -1 and the y-intercept is 4.	This time, since the inequality sign includes "equals," the points on the line will satisfy the inequality and so, the line is solid.
Since the inequality sign is strict, the points on the line do not satisfy the inequality and so are not included in the solution set. To denote this fact, the line is dotted.	The other change is the side of the line that is shaded. The inequality can be written equivalently as $y \ge -x + 4$. Since y is *greater than or equal to* the right side, you now shade above the line instead of below it.
Replacing the equals sign by the original "<" sign gives the equivalent inequality $y < -x + 4$. Since y is *less than* the right side, shade below the line.	The solution set is as follows:
The solution set is as follows:	

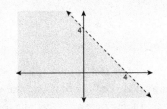

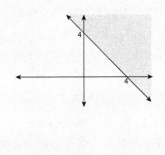

These types of inequalities are used to model certain real-world scenarios. For instance, suppose you have two part-time jobs. One job pays $35 per hour and the other pays $50 per hour. To determine the various combinations of the numbers of hours you would need work at each job to earn more than $4,000, you would need to set up a linear inequality. To this end, let x be the number of hours worked at the first job and let y be the number of hours worked at the second job. The inequality would be $35x + 50y > 4,000$.

Systems of Linear Inequalities

Lastly, we consider solving a system comprised of two such linear inequalities. Doing so is simply a matter of sketching the solution set of each inequality separately, but on the same set of axes. The overlap of the two regions is where both inequalities hold simultaneously and thus is the solution of the system.

Suppose we want to solve the system

$$\begin{cases} 3x - 2y > 2 \\ x + 2y \le -2 \end{cases}$$

First, sketch the graphs of the corresponding lines $3x - 2y = 2$ (dotted) and $x + 2y = -2$ (solid) on the same set of axes:

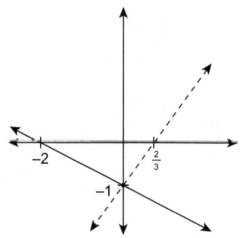

(This is the same graph from the earlier table)

Since the point $(0,0)$ lies on neither line, use it as a test point for determining the solution set for each separate inequality. For the first one, substituting $(0,0)$ into the inequality yields $0 > 2$, a false statement. So, shade on the side of the line that does *not* include $(0,0)$. Similarly, substituting $(0,0)$ into the second inequality yields $0 \le -2$, a false statement. So, shade on the side of the line that does *not* include $(0,0)$. The solution set of the system of inequalities is the intersection of the two shaded areas, as shown here:

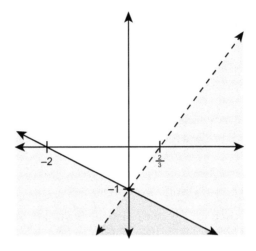

EXPONENTS, LOGARITHMS, AND FINANCIAL LITERACY

Exponential and logarithmic functions arise when modeling important phenomena, such as half-life of radioactive substances, population dynamics, savings account value when interest is compounded continuously, and the measurement of seismic activity. We review the basics of these functions and their main applications, especially to basic finance, in this section.

....

NOTE: Around 22 percent of the questions on the DSST Math for Liberal Arts
exam will cover exponents, logarithms, and financial literacy.

....

Exponential and Logarithmic Functions

Functions of the form $f(x) = A \cdot b^x$, where A is a nonzero real number and b is a positive real number not equal to 1, are called **exponential functions**. The graphs are broken down into two cases depending on b:

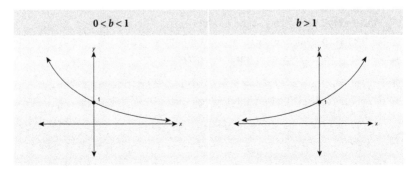

The following are some general observations about exponential functions:

- If $0 < b < 1$, the graph of $y = b^x$ gets very close to the x-axis as the x-values move to the right, and the y-values grow very rapidly as the x-values move to the left.
- If $b > 1$, the graph of $y = b^x$ gets very close to the x-axis as the x-values move to the left, and the y-values grow very rapidly as the x-values move to the right.
- If $b > 0$, then $b^x > 0$, for any value of x. Consequently, the equation $b^x = 0$ has no solutions.
- A common value for b is the irrational number e, which is approximately 2.71828... This value arises in many business applications.

The inverse function (that is, the function obtained by reflecting a given function's graph over the $y = x$ line) of $f(x) = b^x$, $b > 1$, is a function called a **logarithmic function**, which we denote as $g(x) = \log_b x$, where the **base** $b > 1$. The graph looks like this:

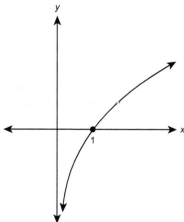

The following are some general observations about logarithmic functions, for any $b > 1$:

- The domain of $g(x) = \log_b x$ is the set of all positive x-values.
- The graph of $y = \log_b x$ plunges sharply as the x-values decrease toward zero, and it grows very slowly as the x-values move to the right.
- If the base b is taken to be the irrational number e, then $\log_b$ is typically written as ln, which stands for **natural logarithm**.

Since $f(x) = b^x$ and $g(x) = \log_b x$ are inverses, the following relationships hold, which are useful when solving equations involving them:

$$\log_b(b^x) = x, \text{ for any real number } x$$

$$b^{\log_b(x)} = x, \text{ for all } x > 0$$

Logarithms and Their Properties

The inverse relationship between exponentials and logarithms gives rise to the following:

$$\log_a b = c \text{ whenever } a^c = b$$

When simplifying expressions involving logarithms, think of $\log_a b$ in the following sense: "To what power must a be raised to get b?" For instance, to simplify $\log_3 9$, identify $a = 3$ and $b = 9$. So, we would ask the question, "To what power must 3 be raised to get 9?" The answer is 2. Similarly, $\log_2 1 = 0$ because $2^0 = 1$.

This also works for fractional exponents. For example, $\log_9 27 = \frac{3}{2}$ because $9^{\frac{3}{2}} = \left(\sqrt{9}\right)^3 = 27$.

There are three main properties used to simplify logarithmic expressions:

Logarithmic Property (in symbols)	Verbal Interpretation
$\log_a M \bullet N = \log_a M + \log_a N$	The logarithm of a product is the sum of the logarithms of the individual factors.
$\log_a \dfrac{M}{N} = \log_a M - \log_a N$	The logarithm of a quotient is the difference of the logarithms of the dividend and divisor (i.e., numerator and denominator).
$\log_a (M^n) = n \log_a M$	The logarithm of the power of a quantity is the power times the logarithm of just the quantity (without the power).

These properties are used to combine arithmetic expressions involving logarithms with the same base into a single logarithm. The following illustrates how these properties are used:

$$\log_7 \frac{2}{49} - \log_7 \frac{2}{7} = \log_7 \left(\frac{2}{49} \div \frac{2}{7}\right)$$
$$= \log_7 \left(\frac{2}{49} \cdot \frac{7}{2}\right)$$
$$= \log_7 \frac{1}{7}$$
$$= -1$$

$$3\log_4 \frac{2}{3} + \log_4 27 = \log_4 \left(\frac{2}{3}\right)^3 + \log_4 27$$
$$= \log_4 \frac{8}{27} + \log_4 27$$
$$= \log_4 \left(\frac{8}{27} \cdot 27\right)$$
$$= \log_4 8$$
$$= \frac{3}{2}$$

The rules can also be used to expand the logarithm of complicated expressions involving powers, products, and quotients, as follows:

$$\log_3 \frac{x^2\sqrt{2x-1}}{(2x+1)^{\frac{3}{2}}} = \log_3\left(x^2\sqrt{2x-1}\right) - \log_3\left(2x+1\right)^{\frac{3}{2}}$$

$$= \log_3\left(x^2\right) + \log_3\underbrace{\sqrt{2x-1}}_{(2x-1)^{\frac{1}{2}}} - \log_3\left(2x+1\right)^{\frac{3}{2}}$$

$$= 2\log_3 x + \frac{1}{2}\log_3(2x-1) - \frac{3}{2}\log_3(2x+1)$$

Beware of common mistakes involving logarithms!

$$\log_a\left(M+N\right) \neq \log_a M + \log_a N$$
$$\log_a\left(M-N\right) \neq \log_a M - \log_a N$$
$$\log_a\left(M+N\right) \neq \log_a M \cdot \log_a N$$
$$\log_a\left(M-N\right) \neq \frac{\log_a M}{\log_a N}$$

The properties are very useful when solving equations involving logarithms. For instance, to solve the equation log $(x + 2) = 2 + $ log $(x - 3)$, proceed as follows:

$$\log(x+2) = 2 + \log(x-3)$$
$$\log(x+2) - \log(x-3) = 2$$
$$\log\left(\frac{x+2}{x-3}\right) = 2$$
$$\frac{x+2}{x-3} = 10^2$$
$$x+2 = 100(x-3)$$
$$x+2 = 100x - 300$$
$$302 = 99x$$
$$x = \frac{302}{99}$$

TIP: You must always verify that the x-values you arrive at actually satisfy the original equation.

Simple and Compound Interest With Investment Applications

When you open a savings account, the two most natural questions to ask are:

- What is the interest rate?
- How often do you compute the interest?

If the interest is computed once at the end of the year, then the interest is characterized as **simple interest**, while it is called **compound interest** if it is computed multiple times per year. The formula for computing such interest is as follows: $V = A\left(1 + \dfrac{r}{n}\right)^{nt}$, where V is the future value of the account after t years, A is the amount deposited into the account, r is the annual interest rate, n is the number of times per year interest is computed (4 if quarterly, 12 if monthly, 52 if weekly, etc.), and t is the number of years you continue to reinvest the amount in the account. If $n = 1$ (that is, the simple interest case), then the **interest earned**, I, after t years is given by the formula $I = Art$.

The following are some typical problems involving simple and compound interest:

Problem	Solution
If you deposit $8,000 into a savings account paying 3% annual interest compounded weekly, what will be the value of the account after 5 years?	Use $V = A\left(1 + \dfrac{r}{n}\right)^{nt}$ with $A = 8,000$, $r = 0.03$, $n = 52$, and $t = 5$. Solve for V. $$V = \$8,000\left(1 + \frac{0.03}{52}\right)^{52(5)}$$ $$= \$9,294.27$$
What amount of money would you need to deposit in an account today at 4% interest compounded quarterly to have $14,500 in the account after 8 years?	Use $V = A\left(1 + \dfrac{r}{n}\right)^{nt}$ with $V = 14,500$, $r = 0.04$, $n = 4$, and $t = 8$. Solve for A. $$\$14,500 = A\left(1 + \frac{0.04}{4}\right)^{4(8)}$$ $$\$14,500 = A\left(1.37494\right)$$ $$\$10,545.90 = A$$

Problem	Solution
If you deposit \$10,000 into an account paying 4% annual interest compounded daily, how many years will it take until the value of the account is \$13,500?	Use $V = A\left(1+\dfrac{r}{n}\right)^{nt}$ with $A = 10,000$, $r = 0.04$, $n = 365$, and $V = 13,500$. Solve for t. $$\$13,500 = 10,000\left(1+\dfrac{0.04}{365}\right)^{365t}$$ $$1.35 = (1.00011)^{365t}$$ $$\log 1.35 = \log(1.00011)^{365t}$$ $$\log 1.35 = (365t)\log(1.00011)$$ $$\dfrac{\log 1.35}{365\log(1.00011)} = t$$ $$7.475 \text{ years } = t$$

Installment Buying, Student Loans, and Home Buying

Whenever you take out a loan—whether it is to pay for school, a car, or a house—a critical question is determining the monthly payment of the loan to ensure you have the means to pay it off. This might seem daunting, but the calculation is not bad at all once you are familiar with the financial jargon. Let us review that first and then jump into the computations.

The **cash price** is the amount of the item (school, house, car, etc.) for which you need the loan. The amount you borrow is the **financed amount** and the amount you pay up-front is the **down payment**. Observe that:

Financed amount = cash price − down payment

You make a down payment as well as fixed monthly payments for a certain number of months. The sum of these is the amount you pay all told and is called the **total installment price**. The total interest that you pay once all is said and done is the **finance charge**. Observe that:

Finance charge = total installment price − cash price

The formula $A = \left(1-\dfrac{1}{(1+i)^{n}}\right) \times \dfrac{R}{i}$, where A is the amount of the loan, R is

the monthly payment, i is the monthly interest rate (= annual interest rate divided by 12), and n is the total number of payments, is used to determine the amount of the loan.

The following is a typical problem involving installment buying:

Problem	Solution
Suppose you purchase a car for $19,500 with a $2,000 down payment at a monthly interest rate of 1.35% for 60 months. What is the monthly payment and what are the total finance charges?	Use $A = \left(1 - \dfrac{1}{(1+i)^n}\right) \times \dfrac{R}{i}$ with $A = \$19{,}500$ $- \$2{,}000$, $i = 0.0135$ and $n = 60$. Solve for R. $$A = \left(1 - \dfrac{1}{(1+i)^n}\right) \times \dfrac{R}{i}$$ $$17{,}500 = \left(1 - \dfrac{1}{(1+0.0135)^{60}}\right) \times \dfrac{R}{0.0135}$$ $$17{,}500 \approx 40.94R$$ $$R \approx \$427.46$$ Next, note that the total installment price is ($427.46) (60) + ($2,000) = $27,647.60. Hence, the finance charge is $27,647.60 − $19,500 = $8,147.60.

COUNTING, PROBABILITY THEORY, AND STATISTICS

This final section is devoted to reviewing some concepts of elementary probability and basic statistics.

....

NOTE: Around 20 percent of the questions on the DSST Math for Liberal Arts exam will test your knowledge of counting, probability theory, and statistics.

....

Permutations and Combinations

There are two systematic ways of counting: permutations and combinations. To begin, a **permutation** of a set of objects is an arrangement of those objects in which each object is used only once and the order in which they are arranged matters. For example, if you have objects labeled A, B, C, and D, both ABCD and DACB are permutations of these objects. Any ordering of the letters produces another permutation. The number of ways to arrange n objects in such a manner is $n!$, where $n! = n \times (n-1) \times (n-2) \times \ldots \times 3 \times 2 \times 1$. (For example, $5! = 5 \times 4 \times 3 \times 2 \times 1$.) Sometimes, we want to only arrange a subset of the objects in set; that is, what if we had n letters but we only wanted to arrange k ($< n$) of them? This is "a permutation of n objects taken k at a time." The number of such arrangements is $P(n,k) = \dfrac{n!}{(n-k)!}$.

The order in which objects are arranged is not always relevant, like when forming a committee of 4 people from a group of 10 people in which all committee members are equally influential in the work being performed, or when simply selecting 4 cards randomly from a standard deck of 52 cards. To determine the number of such selections, we use a **combination**. The "number of combinations of n objects taken k at a time" in which order does NOT matter is computed using the formula $C(n,k) = \dfrac{n!}{k!(n-k)!}$.

For example, let's say a couple wants to try new recipes part of the Paleo diet. They have gathered 15 recipes and want to make 3 for the upcoming week. They like them all equally well so they put them in a box and choose 3 randomly. The number of ways they can make such a selection is $C(15,3)$, since the order in which the recipes are arranged is not relevant.

Fundamentals of Probability

The notion of **chance** pervades real-life. The likelihood of rain, the chance you will win the lottery, how likely is it for a receiver to score a touchdown, etc., are all applications of probability. Addressing these questions requires we establish a method for measuring likelihood. To begin, let us introduce some terminology.

An **outcome** is the result of a single trial of a probability experiment. The collection of all outcomes of an experiment is a set called the **sample space**, labeled as S. For instance, if you roll an eight-sided die (with faces labeled 1, 2, 3, 4, 5, 6, 7, and 8) and record the number of the face on which it comes to rest, the outcomes of the experiment are simply the labels on the faces. So, $S = \{1, 2, 3, 4, 5, 6, 7, 8\}$. An **event** is a subset of the sample space and is usually described by one or more conditions. For instance, the event E that "the die lands on an odd number" is the subset $E = \{1, 3, 5, 7\}$.

The **probability** of an event E, denoted $P(E)$, is a number between 0 and 1, inclusive, that measures the percent chance of the occurrence of event E. How is this number computed? For most experiments you will encounter, each outcome in the sample space is *equally likely*. So, if the sample space contains N outcomes, then the probability of any *one* of them occurring is $\dfrac{1}{N}$. More generally, if event E contains k elements, then

$$P(E) = \frac{\text{Number of outcomes in } A}{\text{Number of possible outcomes}} = \frac{k}{N}.$$

Let's revisit the Paleo diet example. Suppose 4 of the recipes contain quinoa and the couple wants to know the probability that the 3 recipes they select at random all contain quinoa. To compute this probability, first note that the total number of possible outcomes is C (15,3). Also, there are C (4,3) ways of selecting 3 recipes from the 4 quinoa recipes in the collection. Combining these two pieces of information, we conclude:

$$P(\text{all 3 recipes contain quinoa}) = \frac{C(4,3)}{C(15,3)}$$

Sometimes, data from an experiment, like the results of a survey, is in the form of **frequencies**. For instance, say you ask 400 randomly chosen people a series of 10 questions for which each question has 7 possible outcomes. For each question, you would tabulate the frequencies, or number of responses, for each of the 7 choices and divide each by the total number of responses, or 400; the decimals obtained are called **relative frequencies**. They can be used to make educated guesses about how the entire population from which the respondents were chosen would answer such questions.

You have likely heard the question, "What are the *odds* of that event happening?" While it is intuitive that this should be related to computing the probability of the event happening, the manner in which the **odds** of an event occurring is reported is different. Specifically, the odds of event E

$$\text{occurring} = \frac{P(E)}{1 - P(E)}.$$

This is really the ratio, "probability that E occurs *to* probability that E does not occur." As such, the odds of E occurring are often written as $P(E) : (1 - P(E))$. Referring to the Paleo diet example, the odds that all

three recipes chosen contain quinoa are $\dfrac{C(4,3)}{C(15,3)} : 1 - \dfrac{C(4,3)}{C(15,3)}$.

Compound Events

Suppose E and F are events of a probability experiment. Three common **compound events** that can be formed using E and F are as follows:

Event	Description (In Words)
Complement of E	All outcomes NOT in E
E or F	All outcomes in E or in F or in both
E and F	All outcomes in common to E and F

Two events are **mutually exclusive** if they do not share any outcomes.

When computing the probability of the event E or F, we must make certain not to count the outcomes common to both E and F twice. The following **addition formula** comes to the rescue:

$$P(E \text{ or } F) = P(E) + P(F) - P(E \text{ and } F)$$

When E and F are mutually exclusive, $P(E \text{ and } F) = 0$ and so this formula simplifies to $P(E \text{ or } F) = P(E) + P(F)$.

For instance, suppose a children's cereal manufacturer has decided to include two different types of special codes in some of the boxes of cereal it produces for the next three months. The codes can be redeemed online for special prizes. One type of code is included in 10% of all boxes of cereal produced and the second type of code is included in 0.5% of all boxes of cereal produced. Finally, 0.003% of the cereal boxes include *both* types of codes. If a box of cereal is purchased, what is the probability that the box will include at least one type of code?

To answer this question, first note that the event "box contains at least one type of code" represents the event that the box contains the first type of code, the second type of code, or BOTH. So, P("box contains at least one type of code") = P(contains first code OR second code).

Applying the addition rule yields:

P(first code OR second code) = P(first code) + P(second code) − P(first AND second code) = $0.10 + 0.05 - 0.003 = 0.147$

Conditional Probability

Suppose that when computing the probability of an event, you are given an extra piece of information that enables you to restrict your attention to a portion of the sample space. This would impact the probability calculation because the number of possible outcomes has been reduced. A probability like this, where you are given an extra piece of information, is known as a **conditional probability**.

This type of problem occurs on the DSST exam in the form of using a so-called **two-way table**. For example, the table below shows the distribution by gender of 200 voters polled and their answers to the question "Do you prefer a candidate for mayor who prioritizes education reform primarily, or one who prioritizes controlling urban violence?"

Preference of Candidate's Top Priority

	Education Reform	Controlling Urban Violence	TOTAL
Male	45	30	75
Female	60	65	125
TOTAL	105	95	200

Suppose a voter is selected at random from this sample. Depending on the nature of the event for which the probability is sought, the data is used in different ways.

The following are some common questions that can be asked:

Problem	Solution
What is the probability that the voter is male and prefers a candidate who prioritizes controlling urban violence?	**Identify the event:** "male AND urban violence" **Compute probability:** Use only one cell in the table: the one with the entry "30." The probability is $\dfrac{30}{200} = 0.15$.
What is the probability that the voter is either female or prefers a candidate who prioritizes education?	**Identify the event:** "female OR education" **Compute the probability:** This time, you must use the addition formula: $P(\text{female OR education}) =$ $P(\text{female}) + P(\text{education}) - P(\text{female AND education})$. Using the second row yields $P(\text{female}) = \dfrac{125}{200}$. Using the first column yields $P(\text{education}) = \dfrac{105}{200}$. Using the second cell in the first column yields $P(\text{female AND education}) = \dfrac{60}{200}$. So, $P(\text{female OR education}) =$ $\dfrac{125}{200} + \dfrac{105}{200} - \dfrac{60}{200} = \dfrac{170}{200} = 0.85$.

Problem	Solution
What is the probability that the voter prefers a candidate who prioritizes controlling urban violence *given that* the voter is male?	**Identify the event:** This requires computing a conditional probability. The key phrase that tells us this is "given that." **Compute the probability:** The "given that" portion, namely "voter is male," tells us to restrict our attention to the first row of the table. This means we only have 75 outcomes to consider rather than the whole 200. Next, *of these* 75, the number preferring a candidate who prioritizes controlling urban violence is 30. So, the probability is $\frac{30}{75} = 0.4$.

> **TIP:** Be very careful to use the "given that" information to restrict your attention in the table to the appropriate row or column.

Descriptive Statistics

Once data is collected, the next step is to understand the information it conveys. A first line of attack in this regard is using **descriptive statistics**. This includes a set of measures that tell us something about the data.

The **mean** of a numerical data set is the usual arithmetic average of the data values. Just sum the values and divide by *the total number of values* you added. If zero is among the values you included in the sum when finding the mean, you MUST include that value (however many times it occurs) in the total count by which you divide; otherwise, you haven't accounted for its effect on the average.

This measure gives a good idea about the **center** of the data set when there are **no extreme values**, or values that are vastly different from the bulk of the data. But, in a data set like {20, 20, 20, 20, 90}, it is reasonable to think that the "average value" should be 20 since 4 of the 5 values are 20; however, the arithmetic average, or mean, is 34, which is not a good descriptor of the center of this data set! For such a situation, we need a different way of computing "average" or center.

The **median** is another way of computing the center of a data set that is not impacted by the effects of extreme values. To compute the median, arrange the values in the data set from smallest to largest. If there is an odd number of data values, then the median is the data value in the middle of the set. For instance, if there are 29 data values arranged in numerical order, the median is the value in the 15th position (obtained by dividing 29 by 2 and adding 1 to the whole part). If there is an even number of data values, then the median is the arithmetic average of the "middle two" values. For instance, if there are 40 data values arranged in numerical order, then median is the average of the values in the 20th and 21st positions. By definition, half of the data values lie to the left of the median and half lie to its right.

The mean and median are only defined for data sets of numerical values. If the data is **qualitative** in nature (e.g., favorite novel, movie genre preference), then there is no average value. But, we *can* determine which value occurs most often in a data set; this is called the **mode**. For instance, the mode of the data set {horror, comedy, comedy, drama, comedy, horror} is comedy. There can be two values that occur the same number of times and for which this is the greatest frequency; such a data set is **bimodal**. For example, the modes of the data set {7, 9, 7, 7, 2, 4, 9, 9, 3, 4} are 7 and 9. If all values of a data set occur the same number of times, then there is *no mode*.

The above three measures provide no indication as to how the data is **spread out**. For instance, the data sets {20, 20, 20, 20, 20, 20} and {16, 16, 16, 24, 24, 24} both have a mean of 20, but are *very* different. To distinguish between such data sets, there are two commonly used **measures of variability**: standard deviation and interquartile range.

The **standard deviation**, s, is generally used for data sets for which the mean is a good description of its center. This is a measure of the *typical distance* between data values and the mean. The formula for the standard deviation for a data set containing n data values is as follows:

$$s = \sqrt{\frac{\Sigma(x - \text{mean})^2}{n}}$$

Here, x represents a data value. You will not need to compute this for a complicated data set, but you should know that the larger the s value, the more spread out the data.

The **interquartile range**, IQR, is generally used with data sets for which the median best describes the center. This is a measure of the spread of the middle 50% of the data set. To compute the IQR, we must determine the **quartiles**, or data values in the 25th, 50th, and 75th positions in the data set whose values have been arranged from least to greatest. The 2nd quartile is the median. To find the 1st quartile, divide the number of values in the data set by 4. The resulting number is the position of the 1st quartile; to get the value, locate the data value with the position at the *whole* portion of this quotient. The position of the 3rd quartile is obtained by multiplying the position of the 1st quartile by 3; its value is determined in a manner like the 1st quartile.

Finally, the **range** of a data set gives an idea of the overall span of the data values. It is computed by subtracting the smallest data value from the largest one.

Visual Statistics

There are many different types of graphs used to visualize a data set. Let's briefly explore each one below.

A **bar graph** (or **frequency histogram**) is arguably the most basic way of visualizing data; bars of different heights are used to display the frequency of a collection of categories. A **relative frequency histogram** is obtained from a bar graph by simply dividing each bar height by the sum of *all* bar heights of which the graph is composed. So, the height of each bar now represents the percentage of the whole that the bar contributes. Hence, each bar height can be interpreted as the probability that the category would be chosen if a choice were made at random. Whenever the shape of the histogram peaks in the middle and falls symmetrically to the left and right, the mean and median are approximately equal. When it is not symmetric, the mean is pulled toward the tail of the histogram since outliers affect it.

For example, suppose there are 6 candidates vying for the position of student government treasurer. At the beginning of the campaigning period, 50 students are randomly chosen and asked to indicate their top candidate based on information available at that moment in time.

The results are as follows:

Frequency		Relative Frequency	
Candidate	Frequency	Candidate	Frequency
A	6	A	0.12
B	11	B	0.22

C	2	C	0.04
D	8	D	0.16
E	15	E	0.30
F	8	F	0.16

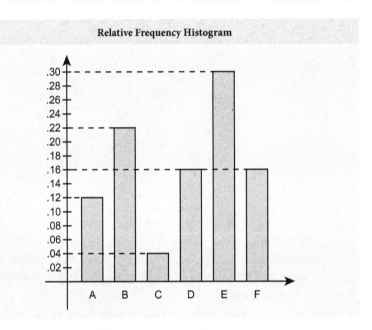

Relative Frequency Histogram

Some questions that could be asked are as follows:

- What is the probability that a randomly selected student favors candidate A?
  (Answer: 0.12)
- What is the probability that a randomly selected student favors either candidate B or D?
  (Answer: 0.22 + 0.16 = 0.48)
- What is the probability that a randomly selected student does not favor candidate E?
  (Answer: 1 − 0.30 = 0.70)

A **pie chart** is a circular graph that is divided into pie-shaped wedges, each representing a percentage of the entire circle. Interpreting the relative frequencies in the above example as percentages, we can form a pie chart to illustrate the data as follows:

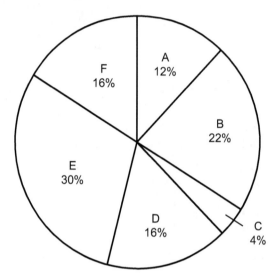

A **dot plot** is a quickly formed bar graph useful for displaying and visualizing small data sets. You decide on a scale and then put a dot above each value along the x-axis; multiple occurrences of values in a data set are represented by stacked dots above that value on the x-axis. For instance, consider the following example:

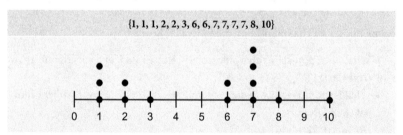

A **line graph** is a graph that consists of a sequence of data points, typically generated in some order dictated by the numerical scale along the x-axis (e.g., time, length, weight, cost), connected by straight line segments. A **trend** is sought in the ebb and flow of the data point heights as a function of the x-axis variable.

For example, a small company logs the number of bags of deer corn (in hundreds) it sells monthly. Its findings are illustrated in the following line graph:

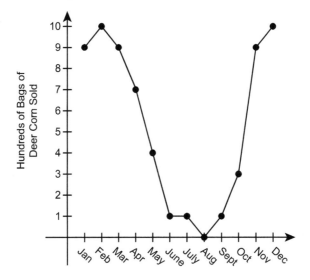

A **box plot** is a way to visualize a numerical data set using five statistics: minimum value, 1st quartile, median, 3rd quartile, and maximum value. The graph consists of two points corresponding to the smallest and largest values in the data set, and three vertical line segments corresponding to the quartiles and median. A box is constructed with the quartiles as two parallel sides, and horizontal line segments are drawn from these two sides to the minimum and maximum values.

For instance, consider the following example:

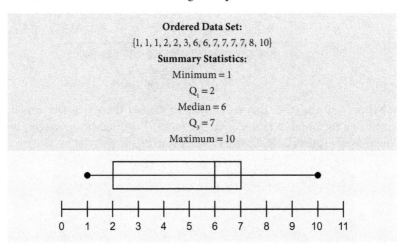

Ordered Data Set:
{1, 1, 1, 2, 2, 3, 6, 6, 7, 7, 7, 7, 8, 10}
Summary Statistics:
Minimum = 1
$Q_1 = 2$
Median = 6
$Q_3 = 7$
Maximum = 10

Rather than eyeballing them, outliers in a data set can be detected using the IQR. Here, IQR = 7 − 2 = 5. An **outlier** is a data value that is *less than* Q_1 − 1.5 × *IQR* or *larger than* Q_3 + 1.5 × *IQR*. For the above example, any value less than 2 − 1.5(5) = −5.5 or greater than 7 + 1.5(5) = 14.5 is an outlier. So, there are no outliers present.

A **scatterplot** is a way of representing data sets consisting of ordered pairs (x, y) on a coordinate plane in order to find the relationship between x and y. The more tightly packed the points are in a scatterplot, the stronger the relationship. If the data points rise from left to right, we say the relationship is *positive*, while if they fall from left to right, we say the trend is *negative*. For example, medical records for a large sample of patients from the past year who were seen for complications due to influenza were used to determine if there might be a relationship between the duration of the flu symptoms and the patient's weight.

The following is a scatterplot illustrating this data:

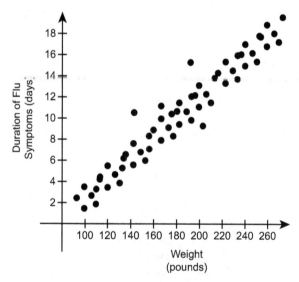

Judging from the data, it is reasonable to suspect there is a relationship between weight and duration of flu symptoms—the higher the weight, the longer it seems to take for the flu symptoms to dissipate.

SUMMING IT UP

- The set of **natural numbers** consists of the numbers 1, 2, 3, 4 ... A natural number other than 1 is **prime** if it can only be written as a product of itself and 1; otherwise, it is **composite**. The GCF of two natural numbers x and y is the *largest* natural number that is a factor of both x and y; the **LCM** of x and y is the *smallest* natural number that is a multiple of both x and y.
- The set of integers is $\{\ldots, -3, -2, -1, 0, 1, 2, 3 \ldots\}$. An even number can be written as $2n$, where n is an integer; an odd number can be written as $2n +1$, where n is an integer.
- If b and n are natural numbers, then $b^n = \underbrace{b \times \ldots \times b}_{n \text{ times}}$. Suppose that $a, b, m,$ and n are all real numbers. There are several rules governing how to work with expressions with exponents.
- A **rational number** is a quotient of two integers, denoted by $\frac{a}{b}$, where $b \neq 0$. Such a fraction is **simplified** if a and b do not share common factors. An **irrational number** is a real number that is not rational, like square roots of prime numbers, π, and e.
- The properties of real numbers—**commutative, associative, distributive,** and **zero factor property**—are useful when simplifying expressions and solving equations.
- **Decimals** are comprised of numerals appearing before and after the decimal point, each of which represents a multiple of a power of 10. The arithmetic of decimals is the same as for natural numbers with the additional step of correctly positioning the decimal point.
- Real numbers that cannot be conveniently written in decimal form are expressed using **scientific notation**: this is the form $m \times 10^n$, where m is a decimal with a single nonzero digit appearing before the decimal point and n is an integer.
- A **percent** is used to express the number of *parts* of a *whole*.
- The **real number line** is a convenient way of illustrating the relative position of real numbers with respect to 0. If $p < q$, then q would be further to the right along the real number line than p.
- Different numeration systems, like **base 2** and **Roman numerals**, have been designed for specific purposes, while others arose as different civilizations' means of communicating numeracy.

- A **logical** statement is a declarative sentence that is *either* true *or* false. It cannot be neither true nor false and it cannot be both true and false. An **open sentence** is any declarative sentence that contains one or more variables. We could ask whether there is some value of the variable for which the statement is true, or whether it is true for all possible values of the variable. This is called **quantifying** the open sentence.
- The truth of any statement is denied by asserting the truth of its **negation**.
- Complex statements can be formed by connecting statements by means of certain words such as *and, or, if … then* called **logical connectives**. Such statements are called **compound statements**.
- The **disjunction** $p \vee q$ is true whenever *at least one* of p, q is true; it is false only when both are false.
- The **conjunction** $p \wedge q$ is true whenever *both* p, q are true; it is false otherwise.
- Compound statements involving one or more constituents $p, q, r...$, are **logically equivalent** provided they have the same truth value for every possible truth assignment to their constituent parts.
- An assertion of the form "if p, then q" (denoted $p \Rightarrow q$) is an **implication**. The statement p is called the **hypothesis** and the statement q is called the **conclusion**. The negation of an implication, $\sim (p \Rightarrow q)$, is logically equivalent to $p \wedge \sim q$.
- A statement of the form "p if and only if q" is called a **biconditional** and is denoted "$p \Leftrightarrow q$."
- **De Morgan's laws** are used to negate disjunctions and conjunctions.
- Given the conditional $p \Rightarrow q$, the **contrapositive** is the conditional $\sim q \Rightarrow \sim p$, and the **converse** is the conditional $q \Rightarrow p$.
- **Proving** a statement is often done by stringing together implications and using the fact that $[(p \Rightarrow r) \wedge (r \Rightarrow q)]$ is logically equivalent to $p \Rightarrow q$.
- A **syllogism** is a collection of statements followed by a conclusion. It is **valid** if whenever the premises are true, the conclusion is true. A pictorial way of determining if a syllogism is valid is by using an **Euler diagram**.
- A **set** is a collection of objects, or **elements**. If $P(x)$ is an open sentence and if A is the set of all objects satisfying $P(x)$, then using **set-builder notation**, we write $A = \{x: P(x)\}$.
- An underlying set that contains all possible elements that any of our sets in the discussion can contain is the **universal set**. A is a **subset** of B and written as $A \subseteq B$ if $x \in A \Rightarrow x \in B$.
- The **complement** of a set A is $\{x : x \in U \text{ and } x \notin A\}$.
- The **union** $A \cup B$ is the set $\{x \in U : x \in A \text{ or } x \in B\}$.
- The **intersection** $A \cap B$ is the set $\{x \in U : x \in A \text{ and } x \in B\}$.
- Different **units of measurement** are used to quantify different types of quantities, like time, speed, liquid measures, length, area, and volume. The **metric system** is based on powers of 10.

- Performing conversions of units of length, area, or volume in the metric system are simple matters of moving the decimal point. **Converting units** in the US customary system is slightly more involved only because the units are not based on powers of 10. The key is to set up products of fractions that show the original units canceling and the new units remaining in the final product.
- The **triangle inequality** says that the sum of the lengths of any two sides of a triangle must be strictly larger than the length of the third side.
- The **triangle sum rule** says that the sum of the measures of the three angles in any triangle must be 180°.
- If the legs of a right triangle are a and b and the **hypotenuse** (side opposite the right angle) is c, then the **Pythagorean theorem** says $a^2 + b^2 = c^2$.
- The **perimeter** of a region in the plane is the "distance around."
- The **area** of a region in the plane is the number of *unit squares* needed to cover it.
- To compute the **surface area** of a solid, the solid is dissected and flattened out so that it can be visualized as a combination of recognizable figures whose areas can be computed using known formulas.
- The **volume** of a solid in space is the number of *unit cubes* needed to fill it.
- A set of rules called the **order of operations** is used to simplify an arithmetic expression involving all types of real numbers and operations.
- A **ratio** is a comparison of a positive quantity x to another positive quantity y expressed as a fraction $x\,y$ or using the notation $x : y$.
- A **proportion** is an equation relating two ratios; it is expressed by equating two fractions.
- The **graph of an equation of two variables** is the collection of all ordered pairs (x,y) in the xy-coordinate plane that satisfy the equation; that is, when the respective values for x and y are substituted into the equation, the result is a true statement.
- A **function** f is a rule that assigns to each element x in one set A exactly one element y, denoted $f(x)$, in another set B. To compute the functional value, substitute the given value in for the variable and simplify the resulting arithmetic expression using the rules of arithmetic.
- The **slope**, m, of the line is defined to be $m = \dfrac{y_2 - y_1}{x_2 - x_1}$ and is an indication of the steepness of the line. The **slope-intercept form** of the equation of a line is $y = mx + b$, where m is the slope of the line and b is the y-coordinate of its y-intercept.
- **Solving linear equations** involves simplifying various expressions using the order of operations, together with the distributive property of multiplication, to isolate the variable on one side of the equation. You must **balance** both sides of the equations.

- Two or more equations considered simultaneously form a **system** of equations. The methods of **elimination, substitution,** and **graphing** can be used to solve systems.
- To determine the solution set of a **linear inequality in two variables,** start by graphing the line (dotted if the inequality sign is > or <, and solid otherwise). Choose a point either above or below the line and see if it satisfies the inequality. If it does, then shade the entire region containing that point on that side of the line; otherwise, shade the entire region on the other side.
- Solving a **system of two linear inequalities in two variables** involves sketching the solution set of each inequality separately, but on the same set of axes. The overlap of the two regions is where both inequalities hold simultaneously and thus is the solution of the system.
- Functions of the form $f(x) = A \cdot b^x$, where A is a nonzero real number and b is a positive real number not equal to 1, are called **exponential functions.** The **inverse function** (that is, the function obtained by reflecting a given function's graph over the $y = x$ line) of $f(x) = b^x$, $b > 1$, is a function called a **logarithmic function,** denoted as $g(x) = \log_b x$, where b is the **base.**
- The inverse relationship between exponentials and logarithms gives rise to $\log_a b = c$ whenever $a^c = b$.
- There are three main **logarithm rules** used for simplifying expressions involving the logarithms of powers, products, and quotients: (1) the logarithm of a product is the sum of the logarithms of the individual factors, (2) the logarithm of a quotient is the difference of the logarithms of the dividend and divisor (i.e., numerator and denominator), and (3) the logarithm of the power of a quantity is the power times the logarithm of just the quantity (without the power).
- When you open a savings account that earns interest, if the interest is computed once at the end of the year, then the interest is characterized as **simple interest,** while it is called **compound interest** if it is computed multiple times per year.
- When taking out a loan, the **cash price** is the amount of the item for which you need the loan. The amount you borrow is the **financed amount** and the amount you pay upfront is the **down payment.** You make a down payment, as well as fixed monthly payments for a certain number of months. The sum of these is the amount you pay all told and is called the **total installment price.**
- A **permutation** of a set of objects is an arrangement of those objects in which each object is used only once and the order in which they are arranged matters. The number of distinct ways in which k of n letters can be arranged in order is $P(n,k) = \dfrac{n!}{(n-k)!}$.

- The number of **combinations of *n* objects taken *k* at a time** where order does not matter is $C(n,k) = \dfrac{n!}{k!(n-k)!}$.
- An **outcome** is the result of a single trial of a probability experiment. The collection of all outcomes of an experiment is a set called the **sample space**, *S*. An **event** is a subset of the sample space and is usually described by one or more conditions. The **probability** of an event *E*, denoted *P*(*E*), is a number between 0 and 1, inclusive, that measures the percent chance of the occurrence of event *E*.
- The **addition formula** is $P(E \text{ or } F) = P(E) + P(F) - P(E \text{ and } F)$.
- Suppose that when computing the probability of an event, you are given an extra piece of information that enables you to restrict your attention to a portion of the sample space. A probability like this is a **conditional probability**.
- The **mean** of a numerical data set is the usual arithmetic average of the data values. The **median** of a data set is a number for which half of the data values lie to its left and half lie to its right. The **mode** is the value in a data set that occurs most frequently. There can be two values that occur the same number of times and for which this is the greatest frequency; such a data set is **bimodal**.
- The **standard deviation** is a measure of the *typical distance* between data values and the mean.
- The **interquartile range (IQR)** is the difference of the 1st and 3rd quartiles.
- A **relative frequency histogram** is obtained from a bar graph by simply dividing each bar height by the sum of *all* bar heights of which the graph is composed.
- A **pie chart** is a circular graph that is divided into pie-shaped wedges, each of which represents a percentage of the entire circle.
- A **dot plot** is a useful for displaying and visualizing small data sets.
- A **line graph** is a graph that consists of a sequence of data points, typically generated in some order dictated by the numerical scale along the *x*-axis (e.g., time, length, weight, cost), connected by straight line segments.
- A **box plot** is a way to visualize a numerical data set using five statistics: minimum value, 1st quartile, median, 3rd quartile, and maximum value. An **outlier** is a data value that *is less than $Q_1 - 1.5 \times IQR$ or larger than $Q_3 + 1.5 \times IQR$*.
- A **scatterplot** is a way of representing data sets consisting of ordered pairs (*x*, *y*) on a coordinate plane. The more tightly packed the points are in a scatterplot, the stronger the relationship. If the data points rise from left to right, we say the relationship is **positive**; if they fall from left to right, we say the trend is **negative**.

Chapter 4

Math for Liberal Arts Post-Test

POST-TEST ANSWER SHEET

1. Ⓐ Ⓑ Ⓒ Ⓓ
2. Ⓐ Ⓑ Ⓒ Ⓓ
3. Ⓐ Ⓑ Ⓒ Ⓓ
4. Ⓐ Ⓑ Ⓒ Ⓓ
5. Ⓐ Ⓑ Ⓒ Ⓓ
6. Ⓐ Ⓑ Ⓒ Ⓓ
7. Ⓐ Ⓑ Ⓒ Ⓓ
8. Ⓐ Ⓑ Ⓒ Ⓓ
9. Ⓐ Ⓑ Ⓒ Ⓓ
10. Ⓐ Ⓑ Ⓒ Ⓓ
11. Ⓐ Ⓑ Ⓒ Ⓓ
12. Ⓐ Ⓑ Ⓒ Ⓓ
13. Ⓐ Ⓑ Ⓒ Ⓓ
14. Ⓐ Ⓑ Ⓒ Ⓓ
15. Ⓐ Ⓑ Ⓒ Ⓓ

16. Ⓐ Ⓑ Ⓒ Ⓓ
17. Ⓐ Ⓑ Ⓒ Ⓓ
18. Ⓐ Ⓑ Ⓒ Ⓓ
19. Ⓐ Ⓑ Ⓒ Ⓓ
20. Ⓐ Ⓑ Ⓒ Ⓓ
21. Ⓐ Ⓑ Ⓒ Ⓓ
22. Ⓐ Ⓑ Ⓒ Ⓓ
23. Ⓐ Ⓑ Ⓒ Ⓓ
24. Ⓐ Ⓑ Ⓒ Ⓓ
25. Ⓐ Ⓑ Ⓒ Ⓓ
26. Ⓐ Ⓑ Ⓒ Ⓓ
27. Ⓐ Ⓑ Ⓒ Ⓓ
28. Ⓐ Ⓑ Ⓒ Ⓓ
29. Ⓐ Ⓑ Ⓒ Ⓓ
30. Ⓐ Ⓑ Ⓒ Ⓓ

31. Ⓐ Ⓑ Ⓒ Ⓓ
32. Ⓐ Ⓑ Ⓒ Ⓓ
33. Ⓐ Ⓑ Ⓒ Ⓓ
34. Ⓐ Ⓑ Ⓒ Ⓓ
35. Ⓐ Ⓑ Ⓒ Ⓓ
36. Ⓐ Ⓑ Ⓒ Ⓓ
37. Ⓐ Ⓑ Ⓒ Ⓓ
38. Ⓐ Ⓑ Ⓒ Ⓓ
39. Ⓐ Ⓑ Ⓒ Ⓓ
40. Ⓐ Ⓑ Ⓒ Ⓓ
41. Ⓐ Ⓑ Ⓒ Ⓓ
42. Ⓐ Ⓑ Ⓒ Ⓓ
43. Ⓐ Ⓑ Ⓒ Ⓓ
44. Ⓐ Ⓑ Ⓒ Ⓓ
45. Ⓐ Ⓑ Ⓒ Ⓓ

46. Ⓐ Ⓑ Ⓒ Ⓓ

47. Ⓐ Ⓑ Ⓒ Ⓓ

48. Ⓐ Ⓑ Ⓒ Ⓓ

49. Ⓐ Ⓑ Ⓒ Ⓓ

50. Ⓐ Ⓑ Ⓒ Ⓓ

51. Ⓐ Ⓑ Ⓒ Ⓓ

52. Ⓐ Ⓑ Ⓒ Ⓓ

53. Ⓐ Ⓑ Ⓒ Ⓓ

54. Ⓐ Ⓑ Ⓒ Ⓓ

55. Ⓐ Ⓑ Ⓒ Ⓓ

56. Ⓐ Ⓑ Ⓒ Ⓓ

57. Ⓐ Ⓑ Ⓒ Ⓓ

58. Ⓐ Ⓑ Ⓒ Ⓓ

59. Ⓐ Ⓑ Ⓒ Ⓓ

60. Ⓐ Ⓑ Ⓒ Ⓓ

MATH FOR LIBERAL ARTS POST-TEST
72 minutes—60 questions

Directions: Carefully read each of the following 60 questions. Choose the best answer to each question and fill in the corresponding circle on the answer sheet. The Answer Key and Explanations can be found following this post-test.

---

1. Determine the GCF and LCM of the set of whole numbers {171, 54, 12}.

   A. GCF = 1; LCM = 2,052
   B. GCF = 2; LCM = 360
   C. GCF = 3; LCM = 360
   D. GCF = 3; LCM = 2,052

2. What is one-fourth of 2^6?

   A. 1^4
   B. 2^3
   C. 2^4
   D. 2^8

3. An Olympic diver performs a dive from a 20-foot high spring-board; the parabola below illustrates the trajectory of her dive:

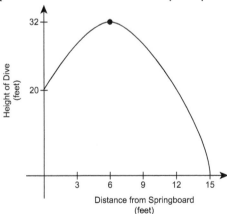

   What is the maximum height of the dive?

   A. 6 feet
   B. 15 feet
   C. 20 feet
   D. 32 feet

4. Which Euler diagram accurately depicts the following syllogism:

Some investments are risky.
College education is an investment.
Therefore, college education can be risky.

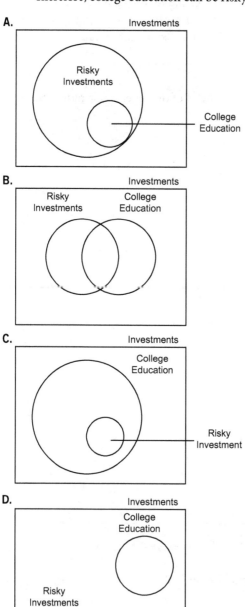

5. Suppose that ln 3 = a and ln 7 = b. Which of the following is equal to ln 63?

A. $2a + 2b$
B. $4b$
C. $2ab$
D. $2a + b$

6. The winner of a semi-annual raffle will receive a paid vacation to the Turks and Caicos Islands. If 10,000 raffle tickets were sold and Henry purchased 40 tickets, what are the odds against him winning the vacation?

A. 40 to 10,000
B. 10,000 to 40
C. 40 to 9,960
D. 9,960 to 40

7. What is the distance, in yards, around a circle with a diameter 18 feet?

A. 3π yards
B. 6π yards
C. 18π yards
D. 36π yards

8. What is the cost (before tax) to purchase carpeting, priced at $8.50 per square yard, to cover the floor of a guest room with dimensions 15 feet by 18 feet?

A. $33
B. $255
C. $270
D. $2,295

9. Which of the following is the solution set of the linear inequality $4x < 6 + 2y$?

A.

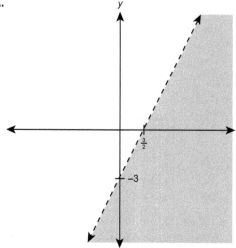

B.

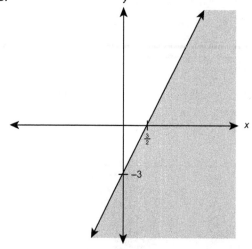

C.

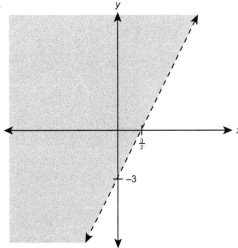

D.

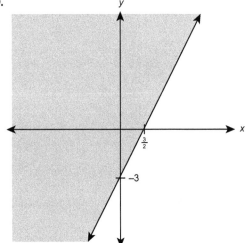

10. To which of the following is the expression $\dfrac{-12z^3x^9}{3x^3z^3}$ equivalent?

A. $-9x^6$

B. $-4x^6$

C. $-9x^3$

D. $-4x^3z$

11. Which property of real numbers does the following illustrate?

$$2.3(1.2) - 2.3(3.4) = 2.3(1.2 - 3.4)$$

A. Distributive property
B. Commutative property
C. Associative property
D. Identity

12. What is the range of the data set {4, 4, 4, 17, 26, 26, 26}?

A. 4
B. 17
C. 22
D. 26

13. In a fantasy novel, a sorcerer found a magic stone whose powers decreased in intensity every day. The table below shows the per-cent-strength of the magic retained by the stone at midnight on several successive days:

Day	Percent-strength of Magic Retained by Stone
1	100%
2	50%
3	25%
4	12.5%

What is the approximate percent-strength of magic retained in the stone on Day 7?

A. 0.0078%
B. 0.78%
C. 1.56%
D. 3.125%

14. What is the product of (4.6×10^3), (6.0×10^{-2}), and (2.0×10^5), expressed using scientific notation?

A. 5.52×10^7
B. 5.52×10^{10}
C. 55,200,000
D. 552,000,000

15. Gina bought her spouse a new watch for his birthday. It comes in a box whose dimensions are 2 inches by 3 inches by 4 inches. How many square inches of wrapping paper does she need to wrap the entire box?

A. 9
B. 24
C. 26
D. 52

16. Find a rational number and an irrational number between $\dfrac{1}{31}$ and $\dfrac{1}{32}$.

A. Rational number = $\dfrac{63}{1,984}$; irrational number = $\dfrac{1}{10\pi}$

B. Rational number = $\dfrac{1}{33}$; irrational number = $\dfrac{1}{10e}$

C. Rational number = $\dfrac{63}{992}$; irrational number = $\dfrac{1}{\pi}$

D. Rational number = $\dfrac{1}{30}$; irrational number = $\dfrac{1}{\sqrt{31}}$

17. You want to deposit $5,000 into a savings account that pays 4% annual interest compounded weekly. What would be the value of n (the number of times per year interest is computed)?

A. 1
B. 4
C. 12
D. 52

18. What type of triangle would have two angles with measures 20° and 80°?

A. Equilateral
B. Scalene
C. Right
D. Isosceles

19. To which of the following equations is $\log_4 z = 2$ equivalent?

A. $z^2 = 4$
B. $2^4 = z$
C. $4^2 = z$
D. $4^z = 2$

20. Consider the Venn diagram pictured below—assume no region is empty:

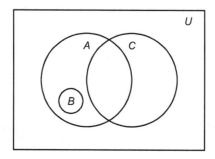

Which of the following statements is false?

A. All members of the set B are also members of set A.
B. Set B and set C are disjoint.
C. Set B is a subset of $A \cup C$.
D. $A \cap C = \emptyset$.

21. Nicole's quiz scores in trigonometry are:
97, 90, 69, 85, 78, 76, 76, 63, 81, 94, 89

Which of the following expresses an accurate relationship between pairs of measures of central tendency?

A. median = mean
B. mode > median
C. mean > mode
D. median > mean

22. Express the following as a decimal:
$5 \times 10^3 + 9 \times 10^0 + 6 \times 10^{-2} + 8 \times 10^{-3}$.

A. 5,009.068
B. 5,900.068
C. 5,090.68
D. 5,009.68

23. To which of the following sets is {x: x is an integer multiple of 4} equivalent?

A. {0, 4, 8, 12, ...}
B. {4, 8, 12, ...}
C. {..., −12, −8, −4, 0, 4, 8, 12, ...}
D. {..., −12, −8, −4, 4, 8, 12, ...}

24. The faces of a fair 6-sided die are labeled as A, C, ←,→,↑, and ↓. If the die is rolled once, which of the following outcomes is the *least* likely to occur?

A. Rolling an arrow
B. Rolling an A or C
C. Not rolling an arrow
D. Rolling an arrow pointing left

25. Which statement could be inserted in the blank so that the conclusion to the following symbolic argument is valid?

$$p \Rightarrow q$$
$$q \Rightarrow r$$

A. $q \Rightarrow p$
B. $p \Rightarrow r$
C. p
D. $\sim p$

26. A common velocity formula is $v = \dfrac{1}{2}gt^2$, where v is velocity, t is time, and g is gravity. Which of the following correctly expresses g in terms of v and t?

A. $g = \dfrac{2v}{t^2}$
B. $g = 2vt^2$
C. $g = \dfrac{2v}{t}$
D. $g = \dfrac{v}{2t^2}$

27. How many different four-letter arrangements are possible using the letters S, P, R, I, N, G if each letter can be used only once?

A. 15
B. 24
C. 360
D. 720

28. Michelle is purchasing a time-share condominium for $100,000. She can secure a loan for 95% of the purchase price at 8% interest for a 25-year term. What would be the amount of her monthly payments under these terms?

A. $557.40
B. $586.73
C. $733.23
D. $771.82

29. Lucas jogged 150 meters in 1.5 minutes. What is his speed in meters per hour?

A. 6 meters per hour
B. 60 meters per hour
C. 100 meters per hour
D. 6,000 meters per hour

30. The gas tank of an SUV holds 18 gallons. When pulling a horse trailer, the SUV travels 100 miles on 3 gallons of gas. Assuming the gas tank is full at the start of the trip, which of the following graphs represents the amount of gas in the tank as a function of the number of miles traveled?

A.

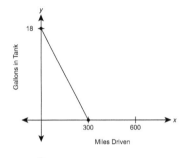

B.

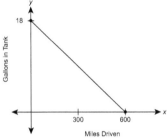

C.

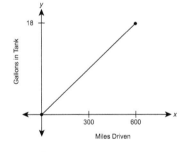

D.

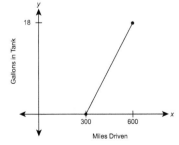

31. The value of a jeep purchased for $20,000 decreases at a rate of 12% annually. What is the value of the car at the end of three years, rounded to the nearest dollar?

A. $28,099
B. $17,600
C. $13,629
D. $12,800

32. An upstart cupcake company conducts a survey at a local mall to determine 300 shoppers' preferences for pistachio, lemon, and chocolate chip cupcakes. The number of shoppers who indicate they like each type of cupcake are indicated in the following Venn diagram:

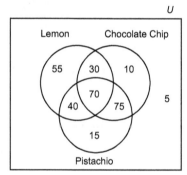

How many shoppers like chocolate chip or pistachio cupcakes, but not lemon?

A. 100
B. 105
C. 240
D. 245

33. Which of the following correctly completes this truth table?

p	q	$\sim p$	$\sim q$	$\sim p \vee \sim q$
T	T			
T	F			
F	T			
F	F			

A.

p	q	$\sim p$	$\sim q$	$\sim p \vee \sim q$
T	T	F	F	F
T	F	F	F	T
F	T	T	T	T
F	F	T	F	T

B.

p	q	$\sim p$	$\sim q$	$\sim p \vee \sim q$
T	T	F	F	F
T	F	F	T	T
F	T	T	F	T
F	F	T	T	T

C.

p	q	$\sim p$	$\sim q$	$\sim p \vee \sim q$
T	T	F	F	T
T	F	F	T	F
F	T	T	F	F
F	F	T	T	F

D.

p	q	$\sim p$	$\sim q$	$\sim p \vee \sim q$
T	T	F	F	F
T	F	F	T	F
F	T	T	F	F
F	F	T	T	T

34. If 1 inch = 2.54 cm, convert 18 cm to inches to the nearest hundredth.

A. 0.14 inches
B. 0.39 inches
C. 7.09 inches
D. 45.72 inches

35. A high school booster club recorded the number of tickets sold for each home basketball game for the current season. The box plot shown represents the data for the number of tickets sold for each game:

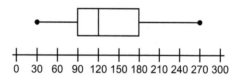

Which conclusion can be made using this graph?

A. The second quartile is 180.
B. The range of tickets sales is 90 to 180.
C. The mean number of tickets sold per game is 120.
D. Twenty-five percent of ticket sales fell between 30 and 90.

36. Peter has gathered 42 medium-sized rocks to use alongside of a walkway. In this group, the number of bluish-gray rocks is three more than twice the number of brown rocks. How many bluish-gray rocks does he have?

A. 13
B. 26
C. 29
D. 36

37. The following line graph shows a distribution of test scores on a college mathematics placement exam.

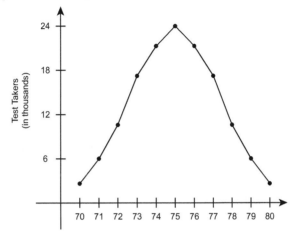

Which of these statements is true based on the graph?

A. The median score and mean score are approximately the same.
B. The graph is comprised of scores from approximately 20,000 test takers.
C. The percentage of scores larger than a given score is the same as the percentage of scores below that same score.
D. More people had a score of 78 than a score of 72.

38. The length of a rectangular room is 5 inches less than three times the width (w) of the room. Which expression is equal to the area of the room?

A. $3w - 5$ square inches
B. $3w^2 - 5w$ square inches
C. $3w^2$ square inches
D. $3w^2 - 5$ square inches

39. What is the base 10 decimal equivalent of the Roman number MMI?

A. 21
B. 101
C. 201
D. 2,001

40. To pay a loan, Allison must make 360 monthly payments of $500 at an 8.5% annual interest rate. To the nearest dollar, what was the original amount of the loan?

A. $2,550
B. $15,300
C. $65,027
D. $70,588.24

41. The probability that it will rain on Tuesday is $\frac{3}{5}$. The probability that it will rain on both Tuesday and Thursday is $\frac{3}{10}$. The probability that it rains on either Tuesday or Thursday is $\frac{4}{5}$. What is the probability that it will rain on Thursday?

A. $\frac{1}{5}$

B. $\frac{1}{2}$

C. $\frac{1}{10}$

D. $\frac{2}{5}$

42. Based on this tabulated information, which of the following formulas describes this function?

x	F(x)
−2	30
−1	10
0	$\frac{10}{3}$
1	$\frac{10}{9}$
2	$\frac{10}{27}$

A. $F(x) = 10 \cdot 3^{-x}$

B. $F(x) = \frac{10}{3} \cdot 3^x$

C. $F(x) = 10 \cdot \left(\frac{1}{3}\right)^{-x}$

D. $F(x) = 10 \cdot 3^{-1-x}$

43. Suppose that A dollars are invested in a money market account that pays i% interest compounded quarterly. What is the value, V, of the account at the end of 10 years?

A. $V = A\left(1 + \dfrac{100i}{4}\right)^{40}$

B. $V = A\left(\dfrac{1+i}{4}\right)^{40}$

C. $V = A\left(1 + \dfrac{i}{400}\right)^{40}$

D. $V = A\left(1 + \dfrac{i}{4}\right)^{40}$

44. What is the negation of the following statement:

"Mario is not older than 25 and Patricia is older than 25."

A. Mario is older than 25 or Patricia is not older than 25.
B. Mario is older than 25 or Patricia is not younger than 25.
C. Mario is older than 25, but Patricia is not older than 25.
D. It is not true that Mario is older than 25 or Patricia is not older than 25.

45. Which of these scenarios describes a negative correlation?

A. The number of quarts of oil purchased and the total amount paid for the oil
B. The amount of gasoline remaining in a truck's tank and the price of gasoline per gallon
C. The size of a truck and the number of gallons of gasoline its tank holds
D. The number of miles driven and the time until the next oil change

46. Teri placed a ladder against the side of her house to clean the rain gutters, as shown below:

Which of the following is the correct expression for x?

A. $x = 20^2 - 18.3^2$
B. $x = 20 - 18.3$
C. $x = \sqrt{20^2 + 18.3^2}$
D. $x = \sqrt{20^2 - 18.3^2}$

47. Suppose that $2,000 was invested at 4% simple interest for 8 years. Which value of r would be substituted into the formula $I = Art$?

A. 0.04

B. 4

C. 8

D. 2,000

48. If $a + ay = b + y$, determine the value of a if $b = -\frac{1}{2}$ and $y = \frac{1}{3}$?

A. $-\frac{1}{8}$

B. $-\frac{1}{2}$

C. $-\frac{3}{2}$

D. $\frac{7}{6}$

49. A tree farm owner examines the relationship between the price he charges for his spruce trees and the number of spruce trees sold weekly. He records this information for one year and calculates the average number of trees sold weekly for each of five different prices. This information is tabulated below:

Price of Spruce Tree	Number Sold Weekly
$50	14
$100	9
$150	15
$200	11
$250	6

Which of the following scatterplots represents this data?

A.

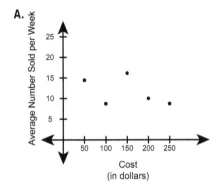

B.

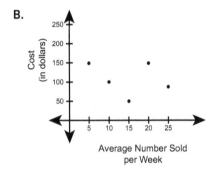

C.

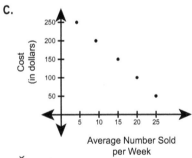

D.

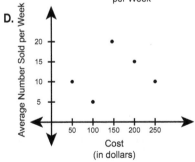

50. What is the equation of the line passing through the points (1,4) and (−2, 2)?

A. $y - 1 = \frac{2}{3}(x - 4)$

B. $y + 1 = \frac{2}{3}(x + 4)$

C. $y - 2 = \frac{2}{3}(x + 2)$

D. $y + 2 = \frac{3}{2}(x - 2)$

51. Which of the following statements is equivalent to the statement, "If you cannot take the heat, stay out of the kitchen?"

A. You can take the heat, but stay out of the kitchen.
B. You can take the heat or stay out of the kitchen.
C. You can take the heat and do not stay out of the kitchen.
D. You cannot take the heat or do not stay out of the kitchen.

52. What is the value of an account at the end of four years if $480 was originally invested at a 10% interest rate compounded quarterly?

A. $320.12
B. $529.83
C. $712.56
D. $1,047.78

53. Consider the following Venn diagram—assume all regions are nonempty:

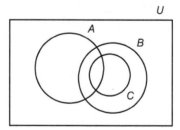

Which one of the following statements is true?

A. No element of the set C is a member of the universal set U.
B. Any element that is a member of the universal set U is also a member of the set A.
C. Some elements of the set A are also elements of the set B.
D. Set B is a subset of set C.

54. The following measurements regarding time and the amount of accumulated snow were taken by a weather aficionado during a storm:

Number of Hours Since the Beginning of the Storm	Number of Inches of Snow Accumulation
0.5	0.75
1	1.50
1.5	2.25
2	3.00
2.5	3.75

What is true about the rate of change of accumulation with respect to time?

A. It is positive.
B. It is negative.
C. It is zero.
D. It is undefined.

55. Suppose U is a universal set for all sets arising in this problem. Which of the following statements is false?

A. For any set, $A \cap A^c = \emptyset$.
B. The set of real numbers is an infinite set.
C. If $A = \{0, 1, 2, 3, 4, 5, ..., 19\}$, then A contains 20 elements.
D. If $B = \{x: x \text{ is an even integer}\}$ and $C = \{y: y \text{ is a multiple of 3}\}$, then B and C are disjoint.

56. Josh invests $1,800 on his 25th birthday in a savings account that earns 7% compounded annually. What will be the value of the account on his 65th birthday? Round your answer to the nearest dollar.

A. $18,974
B. $26,954
C. $50,400
D. $72,000

57. Which equation represents a line perpendicular to the y-axis?

A. $y = 3$

B. $x = 6$

C. $y = x$

D. $y = -x$

58. Use the substitution method to solve the following system of linear equations:

$$\begin{cases} 3x + 2y = -3 \\ 2x - y = 5 \end{cases}$$

A. $3\left(y + \dfrac{5}{2}\right) + 2y = -3$

B. $3\left(\dfrac{5}{2} - y\right) + 2y = -3$

C. $3x + 2(5 - 2x) = -3$

D. $3x + 2(2x - 5) = -3$

59. If \$2,600 is invested in an account that pays 3% simple interest for 5 months, what value of t is substituted into the equation $I = Art$ to compute the interest earned?

A. 0.03

B. 0.05

C. $\dfrac{5}{12}$

D. 5

60. A set C contains 22 elements and a set D contains 35 elements. If $C \cup D$ contains 40 elements, then how many elements does $C \cap D$ contain?

A. 13

B. 17

C. 18

D. 22

ANSWER KEY AND EXPLANATIONS

1. D	13. C	25. B	37. A	49. A
2. C	14. A	26. A	38. B	50. C
3. D	15. D	27. C	39. D	51. B
4. B	16. A	28. C	40. C	52. C
5. D	17. D	29. D	41. B	53. C
6. D	18. D	30. B	42. D	54. A
7. B	19. C	31. C	43. C	55. D
8. B	20. D	32. A	44. A	56. B
9. C	21. C	33. B	45. D	57. A
10. B	22. A	34. C	46. D	58. D
11. A	23. C	35. D	47. A	59. C
12. C	24. D	36. C	48. A	60. B

1. **The correct answer is D.** The largest whole number that divides evenly into all three numbers is 3; this is the GCF. This means choices A and B cannot be correct. The least common multiple is the product $2^2 \times 3^3 \times 19 = 2{,}052$. This eliminates choice C.

2. **The correct answer is C.** Use the exponent rules:

$$\frac{2^6}{4} - \frac{2^6}{2^2} = 2^{6-2} = 2^4$$

Choice A incorrectly divides the bases, which is not part of the exponent rule used to simplify quotients of powers of the same base. Choice B is incorrect because the powers must be subtracted not divided. Choice D is incorrect because you need to subtract the exponents, not add them.

3. **The correct answer is D.** The height of the dive is the y-coordinate of a point on the parabola. The largest that value ever gets is at the vertex, which has a y-coordinate of 32 feet. Choice A is the distance the diver is from the springboard when she achieves the maximum height of her dive (the x-coordinate of the vertex). Choice B is how far she is when she hits the water; so, it is the maximum distance traveled from the springboard. Choice C is the height of the springboard.

4. **The correct answer is B.** The set "Risky Investments" is a subset of the universal set "Investments." The set "College Education" can be risky or not risky, depending on the school, if the major is marketable, etc. So, it should intersect, but not be entirely contained within, the set "Risky Investments." This is shown in the Euler diagram in choice B. Choice A is incorrect because a college education may not be risky if the major is very marketable and one has a full scholarship, for instance. Choice C is incorrect because not every risky investment deals with getting a college education; for instance, investing in a startup company would be a risky investment. Choice D is incorrect because "Risky Investments" should be a set, not a single point, since there are a variety of them.

5. **The correct answer is D.** Use the logarithm properties:

$$\ln 63 = \ln(3^2 \times 7) = \ln(3^2) + \ln 7 = 2\ln 3 + \ln 7 = 2a + b$$

Choice A is equal to $\ln 441$, choice B is equal to $\ln 7^4$, and choice C is equal to $2(\ln 3)(\ln 7)$.

6. **The correct answer is D.** Let A be the event "winning the vacation." Then, A^C is the event "not winning the vacation." The odds of A^C occurring are $P(A^C)$ to $1 - P(A^C)$. Since $P\!\left(A^C\right) = \dfrac{9{,}960}{10{,}000}$ and $1 - P\!\left(A^C\right) = \dfrac{40}{10{,}000}$, the odds are $\dfrac{9{,}960}{10{,}000}$ to $\dfrac{40}{10{,}000}$.

An equivalent way of expressing the ratio is as the fraction

$$\frac{\frac{9{,}960}{10{,}000}}{\frac{40}{10{,}000}} = \frac{9{,}960}{40},$$

which is equivalent to "9,960 to 40." Choice A is incorrect because you must subtract 40 from 10,000, and the ratio is written in the wrong order. Choice B is incorrect because you must subtract 40 from 10,000. Choice C is expressed in the wrong order.

7. **The correct answer is B.** The radius of the circle is 9 feet. This is equivalent to 3 yards. So, the circumference (in yards) is $2\pi(3$ yards$) = 6\pi$ yards. Choice A is incorrect because you need to multiply by 2 in the circumference formula. Choice C is incorrect because you did not convert the diameter to yards. Choice D is incorrect because you used the diameter, as originally expressed in feet, instead of the radius expressed in yards.

8. **The correct answer is B.** First, convert the dimensions to yards. So, the room is 5 yards by 6 yards. The area is 30 square yards. Multiply this by $8.50 (the cost per square yard) to get the pre-tax price: $8.50(30) = $255. Choice A is the result of adding the width to the length; this is not related to the area. Choice C is the area in square feet. Choice D is the result of not converting feet to yards before computing the price.

9. **The correct answer is C.** First, the equation of the corresponding line in slope-intercept form is $y = 2x - 3$. Graph it on the xy-plane as a *dotted* line since the inequality is strict. Next, since $(0,0)$ satisfies the inequality, shade the side of the line containing it— namely above it. The wrong side of the line is shaded in choice A. The line in choices B and D should be dashed, not solid.

10. **The correct answer is B.** Use the exponent rules as follows:

$$\frac{-12z^3x^9}{3x^3z^3} = \frac{-12}{3} \cdot \frac{x^9}{x^3} \cdot \frac{z^3}{z^3}$$
$$= -4 \cdot x^{9-3} \cdot 1$$
$$= -4x^6$$

Choice A is the result of adding the coefficients instead of dividing them. Choice C is the result of adding the coefficients instead of dividing them plus dividing by the powers of x instead of subtracting. Choice D is the result of dividing by the powers of x instead of subtracting, and not canceling the z-terms completely.

11. **The correct answer is A.** The numbers demonstrate the distributive property, which shows how to multiply a quantity by a sum or difference. The communicative property (choice B) governs the order in which real numbers are added or multiplied. The associative property (choice C) governs the way terms of a sum or product are grouped. Identity (choice D) says that if you add 0 to a real number or multiply it by 1, you get the same number back.

12. **The correct answer is C.** The range of a data set is the difference between the maximum and minimum values. Here, this difference is $26 - 4 = 22$. Choice A is the minimum of the data set. Choice B is the median of the data set. Choice D is the maximum of the data set.

13. **The correct answer is C.** Each cell is $\frac{1}{2}$ the value of the one directly above it. So, to get the percent-strength for Day 5, divide the percent-strength for Day 4 by 2 to get 6.25%. Then divide again to find that the percent-strength for Day 6 is 3.125%. And finally, divide once more to get 1.56% as the percent-strength for Day 7. Choice A is the result of an incorrect calculation of the percent-strength for Day 8. Choice B is the percent-strength for Day 8. Choice D is the percent-strength for Day 6.

14. **The correct answer is A.** Multiply by grouping the decimal parts together and the powers of ten together (which is valid by the associative and commutative properties): $(4.6 \times 10^3) \times (6.0 \times 10^{-2}) \times (2.0 \times 10^5) = (4.6 \times 6.0 \times 2.0) \times (10^3 \times 10^{-2} \times 10^5) = 55.2 \times 10^6 = 5.52 \times 10^7$. Choice B is the result of inadvertently using 2 in place of the exponent −2 when computing the power of 10. Choice C is not expressed using scientific notation, even though the result is equivalent. Choice D is not expressed using scientific notation, and the power of 10 used to find this value is wrong.

15. **The correct answer is D.** Compute the surface area of the box by doubling the area of the three distinct faces. Doing so yields $2(2 \bullet 3) + 2(2 \bullet 4) + 2(3 \bullet 4) = 52$ square inches. This is the amount of wrapping paper Gina needs. Choice A is simply the sum of the three given dimensions, which is not related to the surface area. Choice B is the volume. Choice C is half the surface area; do not forget to double the area of each of the three distinct faces.

16. **The correct answer is A.** The average of $\frac{1}{31}$ and $\frac{1}{32}$ is $\frac{63}{1,984}$.

This is a rational number halfway between $\frac{1}{31}$ and $\frac{1}{32}$. Also, 10π
$= 10(3.14) = 31.4$. Hence, $31 < 10\pi < 32$, their reciprocals satisfy

the reverse inequality: $\frac{1}{31}$. The fraction $\frac{1}{10\pi}$ is a quotient of a

nonzero rational number and an irrational number. So, it must

be irrational, as needed. Choice B is incorrect because $\frac{1}{33}$ is not

between $\frac{1}{31}$ and $\frac{1}{32}$. Choices C and D are incorrect because nei-

ther of the given numbers in each answer is between $\frac{1}{31}$ and $\frac{1}{32}$.

17. **The correct answer is D.** The question indicates that interest is computed weekly, so the value of n would be 52. Choice A would be simple interest, choice B is quarterly, and choice C is monthly.

18. **The correct answer is D.** The sum of the three angles of a triangle is 180 degrees. So, the measure of the missing angle is $180 - (20 + 80) = 80$ degrees. Since two angles are congruent, the triangle is isosceles. An equilateral triangle (choice A) would require all three angles to be 60 degrees. A scalene triangle (choice B) would require all three angles to be different. A right triangle (choice C) requires one of the angles to measure 90 degrees, which is not the case.

19. **The correct answer is C.** Use the fact that $\log_b x = y$ is equivalent to $b^y = x$ to see that the given equation is equivalent to $4^2 = z$. Choice A has the z and 4 interchanged. Choice B would be equivalent to $\log_z z = 4$. Choice D has the z and 2 interchanged.

20. **The correct answer is D.** Since all regions are assumed to be nonempty and there is an overlapping region of sets A and C, their intersection cannot be empty. Choice A is a true statement because the circle representing set B is entirely included inside of the circle representing set A. Choice B is true because the circles representing sets B and C do not overlap. Choice C is true because the circle representing set B is entirely inside the region that is comprised of sets A and C.

21. The correct answer is C. First, arrange the data in numerical order:

$$63, 69, 76, 76, 78, 81, 85, 89, 90, 94, 97$$

The mode is the most frequently occurring value: 76. The median is the middle value, which is the one in the 6th position: 81. The mean is the sum of the values divided by 11: approximately 81.6. So, it is evident that the only true statement of those listed is choice C.

22. The correct answer is A. Using the standard base 10 place-value chart, this arithmetic expression is equal to 5,009.068. All other choices are the result of misinterpreting the relationship between the power of 10 and the position of its multiple in the place-value chart.

23. The correct answer is C. An *integer* multiple of 4 has the form $4n$, where n is any integer. You must include the natural numbers, zero, and the negatives of the natural numbers. The only set that includes all these possibilities for n is the one in choice C. Choice A does not account for negative multiples of 4. Choice B does not account for 0 or negative multiples of 4. Choice D neglects to include 0.

24. The correct answer is D. Since the die is fair, it is equally likely for the die to land on any of the six faces. Observe that P (an arrow) = $\frac{4}{6}$, P (rolling an A or C) = $\frac{2}{6}$, P (not rolling an arrow) = $\frac{2}{6}$, and P (rolling an arrow pointing left) = $\frac{1}{6}$. So, this last event is the least likely to occur.

25. The correct answer is B. By stringing together the two conditionals using statement q as a common link, the only logical conclusion one can make from these two statements is that $p \Rightarrow r$. There is not enough information to conclude any of the other statements.

26. The correct answer is A. Solve for g as follows:

$$v = \frac{1}{2}gt^2$$
$$2v = gt^2$$
$$\frac{2v}{t^2} = g$$
$$g = \frac{2v}{t^2}$$

27. The correct answer is C. This question requires that we determine the number of permutations of 6 letters taken 4 at a time—order matters here since we are forming "words." This number is $\frac{6!}{(6-4)!} = \frac{6!}{2!} = 6 \times 5 \times 4 \times 3 = 360$. Choice A is the number of combinations of 6 letters taken 4 at a time, but order matters here. Choice B is just the product of the number of letters from which to choose and the 4 you *want* to choose; it has nothing to do with the number of permutations. Choice D is the number of ways to arrange 6 distinct objects in order; you did not take 4 of them to arrange.

28. The correct answer is C. Use the formula $A = \left(1 - \frac{1}{(1+i)^n}\right) \times \frac{R}{i}$ with $A = 100,000(0.95) = 95,000$, $i = 0.08/12$, and $n = 25(12) = 300$. You want to determine the value of R:

$$95,000 = \left(1 - \frac{1}{\left(1 + \frac{0.08}{12}\right)^{300}}\right) \times \frac{R}{\left(\frac{0.08}{12}\right)}$$
$$733.23 = R$$

So, the monthly payment is \$733.23. Choice A is the result of using a *plus* instead of the *minus* in the formula $A = \left(1 - \frac{1}{(1+i)^n}\right) \times \frac{R}{i}$. Choice B is the result of using a *plus* instead of the *minus* in the formula $A = \left(1 - \frac{1}{(1+i)^n}\right) \times \frac{R}{i}$ and used $A = 100,000$ instead of 95,000. Choice D is the result of $A = 100,000$ instead of 95,000.

29. **The correct answer is D.** Use the fact that 1 hour = 60 minutes to perform the following unit conversion:

$$\frac{150 \text{ meters}}{1.5 \text{ minutes}} = \frac{150 \text{ meters}}{1.5 \ \cancel{\text{minutes}}} \times \frac{60 \ \cancel{\text{minutes}}}{1 \text{ hour}}$$
$$= 6,000 \text{ meters per hour}$$

Choices A and B are off by power(s) of 10, likely due to an arithmetic error. Choice C is the result of assuming there are 10 minutes in an hour rather than 60.

30. **The correct answer is B.** As the distance traveled increases, the amount of gasoline remaining in the tank decreases. So, the line describing this relationship should have a negative slope, meaning it slants downward from left to right. This eliminates choices C and D. Both lines in choices A and B have the correct y-intercept of 18 gallons. However, choice A cannot be correct because the x-intercept should be 600 gallons (not 300) since this is the number of miles the SUV can travel before it runs out of gas.

31. **The correct answer is C.** Use the formula $V = A\left(1 + \dfrac{r}{n}\right)^{nt}$ with $A = 20{,}000$, $r = -0.12$ (negative since the value is decreasing), $n = 1$ (since the decrease is annual), and $t = 3$. The value of the jeep, V, at the end of 3 years is

$$V = \$20{,}000\left(1 + \frac{-0.12}{1}\right)^{1(3)}$$
$$= \$20{,}000(0.88)^3$$
$$= \$13{,}629.40$$

which we round to $13,629. Choice A is the result of using $r = 0.12$ instead of -0.12, which indicates that the value is increasing with time. Choice B is the value at the end of 1 year, not 3. Choice D is the result of incorrectly computing the parenthetical quantity in $V = A\left(1 + \dfrac{r}{n}\right)^{nt}$.

32. **The correct answer is A.** Add the numbers in the three regions in the sets representing chocolate chip cupcakes and pistachio cupcakes that do *not* overlap the region representing lemon cupcakes: $10 + 15 + 75 = 100$. The answer in choice B includes the 5 shoppers who liked none of these three types of cupcakes. The answer in choice C does not exclude the shoppers who like lemon cupcakes from the total. The answer in choice D does not exclude the shoppers who like lemon cupcakes from the total, and included the 5 shoppers who liked none of these three types of cupcakes.

33. **The correct answer is B.** This is the correct truth table because it uses the facts that the truth value of the negation of a statement is the opposite of the truth value of the statement itself. The truth value of a disjunction is true if at least one of the statements used to form it is true and is false if both are false. The table in choice A does not solve for the negation of q correctly. Choice C has the last column wrong; these are the truth values for the negation of the given disjunction. Choice D is the truth table for the conjunction $\sim p \wedge \sim q$.

34. **The correct answer is C.** Convert the units as follows:

$$18 \text{ cm} = 18 \ \cancel{cm} \ \times \frac{1 \text{ inch}}{2.54 \cancel{cm}} = 7.09 \text{ inches}$$

Choice A is the result of dividing in the wrong order. Choice B is the number of inches in 1 cm, not 18 cm. Choice C is the result of multiplying instead of dividing when converting the units.

35. **The correct answer is D.** The first quartile is represented by the vertical line segment at 90. So, 25% of the data lie between the minimum value 30 and 90. Choice A is incorrect because the second quartile is 120 and the third quartile is 180. The answer in choice B would be used to get the interquartile range, not the range. Choice C is incorrect because we can only deduce that the median is 120; since the data set is skewed, evidenced by the fact that the median is not in the middle of the box, it is likely that the mean is not 120.

36. The correct answer is C. Let x be the number of brown rocks. Then, there are $3 + 2x$ bluish-gray rocks. Summing these gives 42: $x + (3 + 2x) = 42$. Solve for x:

$$3x + 3 = 42$$

$$3x = 39$$

$$x = 13$$

So, there are $(3 + 2(13)) = 29$ bluish-gray rocks. Choice A is the number of brown rocks. Choice B is the result of forgetting to add 3; this assumes the number of bluish-gray rocks is twice the number of brown rocks. Choice D is the result of solving $3x = 39$ by subtracting 3 from both sides instead of dividing by 3.

37. The correct answer is A. Since the shape of the graph is symmetric, the median and mean scores are approximately the same. Choice B reflects not computing the total number of test takers correctly; the y-coordinates of all the points on the line graph need to be added. Choice C is true for the 2nd quartile or median, not for every score. Choice D is incorrect since the y-coordinates of the points for which $x = 72$ and $x = 78$ are the same.

38. The correct answer is B. If w is the width of the room, then the length is $3w - 5$. The area is the product of width and length, namely $w(3w - 5) = 3w^2 - 5w$ square inches. Choice A is the length only. The answer in choice C assumes the length is three times the width, not 5 less than this quantity. Choice D is the result of not using the distributive property when multiplying $w(3w - 5)$.

39. The correct answer is D. In Roman numerals, M stands for 1,000 and I stands for 1. There are two Ms, which equates to 2,000. Adding 1 to this number yields 2,001. The answer in choice A mistakenly equates M to 10 instead of 1,000. The answer in choice B mistakenly equates M to 50 instead of 1,000. The answer in choice C mistakenly equates M to 100 instead of 1,000.

40. The correct answer is C. Use the formula $A = \left(1 - \dfrac{1}{(1+i)^n}\right) \times \dfrac{R}{i}$

with $i = \dfrac{0.085}{12}$, $n = 360$, and $R = \$500$. The value of A is the original amount of the loan:

$$A = \left(1 - \frac{1}{\left(1+\dfrac{0.085}{12}\right)^{360}}\right) \times \frac{\$500}{\left(\dfrac{0.085}{12}\right)} = \$65,027$$

Choice A is the result of using the simple interest formula, which does not apply to this scenario. Choice B is the product of n, R, and i, which is not the correct formula. Choice D is just the $\dfrac{R}{i}$ portion of the formula $A = \left(1 - \dfrac{1}{(1+i)^n}\right) \times \dfrac{R}{i}$.

41. The correct answer is B. Use the addition formula:

P(rain on Tues. or rain on Thurs.) = P(rain on Tues.) + P(rain on Thurs.) − P(rain on Tues. and rain on Thurs.)

Substituting the given information into this formula yields the following:

$$\frac{4}{5} = \frac{3}{5} + P(\text{rains on Thurs}) - \frac{3}{10}$$

Now, solve for P(rains on Thurs.) to obtain

$$P(\text{rains on Thurs}) = \frac{4}{5} - \frac{3}{5} + \frac{3}{10} = \frac{1}{2}$$

Choice A is the result of not subtracting P (rain on Tues. and rain on Thurs.), as required by the addition formula. Choices C and D are the results of arithmetic errors involving fractions.

42. The correct answer is D. Substituting the x-values in the left column of the table into each of the functions reveals that choice D gives the correct formula. All other choices have an exponent or base of the exponential portion of the formula wrong.

43. The correct answer is C. Use the formula $V = A\left(1 + \dfrac{r}{n}\right)^{nt}$ with

$r = \dfrac{i}{100}$ (which is the correct conversion of $i\%$), $n = 4$, and $t = 10$

to get

$$V = A\left(1 + \dfrac{\frac{i}{100}}{4}\right)^{4(10)} = A\left(1 + \dfrac{i}{400}\right)^{40}$$

The answer in choice A has 100 in the numerator of the fraction, but it should be in the denominator. Choice B is the result of incorrectly dividing the 1 in the parentheses by n, and converts $i\%$ to a fraction incorrectly. Choice D is the result of converting $i\%$ to a fraction incorrectly.

44. The correct answer is A. Symbolically, the given statement is the conjunction $(\sim p) \wedge q$, where p is the statement "Mario is older than 25" and q is the statement "Patricia is older than 25." Use De Morgan's laws, together with the Law of the Double Negative, to form the negation:

$$\left[(\sim p)\right] \wedge q \equiv \left[\sim(\sim p)\right] \vee (\sim q) \equiv p \vee (\sim q)$$

This is equivalent to the disjunction, "Mario is older than 25 or Patricia is not older than 25." Choice B should have the word "younger" replaced by "older." Choice C is incorrect because the word *but* is semantically equivalent to an *and*. Choice D is equivalent to the given statement, not its negation.

45. The correct answer is D. As the number of miles driven increases, the number of miles until the next oil change decreases. This describes a negative correlation. Choice A does not describe a negative correlation since as you buy more oil, the total amount paid will increase regardless of the price. The answer in choice B would likely have neither a negative nor a positive correlation. Choice C describes what is probably a positive relationship between two variables since the larger the truck, the larger the gas tank (though it may not be linear).

46. **The correct answer is D.** Use the Pythagorean theorem with legs having lengths 18.3 and x and hypotenuse being 20: $x^2 + 18.3^2 = 20^2$. Solve for x as follows:

$$x^2 = 20^2 - 18.3^2$$
$$x = \sqrt{20^2 - 18.3^2}$$

Choice A needs to have a radical on the right side. Choice B is the result of incorrectly saying the radical of a difference is the difference of the radicals. Choice C should have a minus instead of a plus inside the radicand.

47. **The correct answer is A.** In the formula, r is the interest rate expressed as a decimal. Since 4% = 0.04, r must be 0.04. Choice B did not convert 4% to a decimal. Choice C is the value of t. Choice D is the value of A.

48. **The correct answer is A.** Substitute the given values of b and y into the equation and solve for a, as follows:

$$a + a\left(\frac{1}{3}\right) = \frac{1}{2} + \frac{1}{3}$$
$$\frac{4}{3}a = -\frac{1}{6}$$
$$a = -\frac{1}{6} \times \frac{3}{4}$$
$$a = -\frac{1}{8}$$

In choice B, the coefficients of the a-terms are not added correctly; the coefficient of a should be $\frac{4}{3}$, not $\frac{1}{3}$. In choice C, the coefficient of a is subtracted from both sides rather than dividing by it when solving for a. Choice D is the result of multiplying both sides of the equation by the coefficient of a rather than dividing by it when solving for a.

49. **The correct answer is A.** Plotting the points given in the table by identifying the values in the first column as x-values and the values in the second column as the y-values yields the scatterplot in choice A. None of the other scatterplots plot the points correctly.

50. The correct answer is C. The slope of the line is $m = \dfrac{4-2}{1-(-2)} = \dfrac{2}{3}$.

Using the point $(-2,2)$, the equation of the line using point-slope form is $y - 2 = \dfrac{2}{3}\left(x - (-2)\right)$, which simplifies to $y - 2 = \dfrac{2}{3}(x + 2)$. Choice A is the result of interchanging the x- and y-values of the point $(1,4)$ when writing the equation in point-slope form. Choice B is the result of interchanging the x- and y-values of the point $(1,4)$ when writing the equation in point-slope form; they should have been subtracted from x and y in the equation, respectively, rather than added. Choice D has the wrong slope (it should be the reciprocal) and interchanges the x- and y-values of the point $(-2,2)$ when writing the equation in point-slope form.

51. The correct answer is B. Let p be the statement "You can take the heat" and q be the statement "Stay out of the kitchen." The given conditional can be written symbolically as $(\sim p) \Rightarrow q$. But, this is equivalent to $p \vee q$. In words, this is equivalent to, "You can take the heat or you stay out of the kitchen." Choices A and C are conjunctions, but the conditional is equivalent to a disjunction. Choice D should have both statements of which the disjunction is comprised be replaced by their negations.

52. The correct answer is C. Use the formula $V = A\left(1 + \dfrac{r}{n}\right)^{nt}$ with $A = \$480$, $r = 0.10$, $n = 4$, and $t = 4$ to obtain

$$V = \$480\left(1 + \frac{0.10}{4}\right)^{4(4)}$$
$$= \$480(1.025)^{16}$$
$$= \$712.56$$

Choice A is the result of subtracting instead of adding $\dfrac{r}{n}$ in the formula $V = A\left(1 + \dfrac{r}{n}\right)^{nt}$. Choice B is the result of using the wrong exponent in the formula $V = A\left(1 + \dfrac{r}{n}\right)^{nt}$. Choice D is the result of using $n = 2$ instead of 4.

53. **The correct answer is C.** Since all regions are assumed to be nonempty and the circles representing sets A and B overlap, then some elements of A are also elements of B. Choice A is incorrect because the universal set contains all sets within a given discussion. Choice B means that the universal set U is a subset of A, but the opposite is true. (This can only happen if $A = U$.) Choice D has the relationship backwards; set C is a subset of B.

54. **The correct answer is A.** Note that the values in the right column increase by 0.75 for every increase by 0.5 in the left column. This implies the relationship is linear. Moreover, since the values are increasing, the rate of change is positive. As such, all other choices are not viable.

55. **The correct answer is D.** Sets B and C have *infinitely many* elements in common; all multiples of 6 belong to both. Choice A is true since an object cannot both be inside and not inside a set. Choice B is true since, for instance, the set of natural numbers belongs to the set of real numbers and there are clearly infinitely many natural numbers since there is no end to counting. Choice C is true as can be seen by simply counting the elements.

56. **The correct answer is B.** Use the formula $V = A\left(1 + \dfrac{r}{n}\right)^{nt}$ with $A = \$1,800$, $r = 0.07$, $n = 1$, and $t = 40$ to obtain

$$V = \$1,800\left(1 + \frac{0.07}{1}\right)^{1(40)}$$
$$= \$1,800(1.07)^{40}$$
$$= \$26,954$$

Choice A is the result of incorrectly using $r = 0.4$ and $t = 7$. Choice C is the product of 1,800, 40, and 0.7. Choice D is the product of $\$1,800$ and 40, which is not how you compute the value of an account at the end of 40 years.

57. **The correct answer is A.** A line perpendicular to the y-axis must be horizontal. Horizontal lines have equations of the form $y = a$, where a is a real number. The only choice that satisfies this condition is $y = 3$. Choice B is parallel to the y-axis. Choices C and D are diagonal lines through the origin, neither of which intersects the y-axis in a ninety-degree angle.

58. **The correct answer is D.** Solve the second equation for y to get $y = 2x - 5$. Substitute this in for y in the first equation to get $3x + 2(2x - 5) = -3$. Choice A should have the y inside the parentheses being divided by 2. Choice B has the wrong expression inside the parentheses; it should be a sum and the y should be divided by 2. Choice C has the difference inside the parentheses written in the wrong order.

59. **The correct answer is C.** In this formula, t represents the number of *years* of the investment. Be careful—the given number of *months* is 5. This is $\frac{5}{12}$ of a year. Choice A is the interest rate, and so it is the value of r, not t. Choice B is equal to $\frac{5}{100}$, but this is the wrong conversion of months to years; divide 5 by 12, not 100. Choice D is expressed in months, not years, as the formula requires.

60. **The correct answer is B.** Of the total 57 elements that comprise sets C and D, 17 must be in common since otherwise their union would have more than 40 elements. Choice A is the difference of the number of elements in C and D. Choice C would imply that $C \cup D$ contains 39 elements, not 40. Choice D would imply that C is a subset of D, which is not assumed; moreover, $C \cup D$ would not include 40 elements in such case.

Like what you see? Get unlimited access to Peterson's full catalog of DSST practice tests, instructional videos, flashcards, and more for **75% off the first month!** Go to **www.petersons.com/testprep/dsst** and use coupon code **DSST2020** at checkout. Offer expires July 1, 2021.

Printed in the USA
CPSIA information can be obtained
at www.ICGtesting.com
JSHW012037140824
68134JS00033B/3108

9 780768 944624